# FOREST AND TRIBAL LIFE

## [Study of a Micro-Region]

## About the Authors

**Rohit Shukla** (*b.* 1939) is working as Professor of Economics, Sardar Patel Institute of Economic and Social Research, Ahmedabad. His research interests include droughts and famines and rural poverty, social forestry and wasteland development and tribal development in the general theme of agricultural economics. He has published a large number of articles in national and international journals as well as books in English and Gujarati.

**Ambubhal T. Desai** (*b.* 1932) is working as Pro-Vice-Chancellor, Gujarat University, Ahmedabad. His main research interests are rural studies and geography of education. He has published several textbooks and articles on Geography and reviewed and guided a number of dissertations.

**A.B. Vora** (*b.* 1933) is Professor and Head of Botany Department, Gujarat University. His main field of specialization is ecology environmental biology, including air and water, soil pollution eco-physiology, salt, stress, palaeo-ecology and palaeo-climatic. He has to his credit over 125 publications in national and international academic journals.

**R.B. Lal** (*b.* 1935) is working as a Senior Faculty in Tribal Research and Training Institute of Gujarat Vidyapeeth, Ahmedabad. He has a wide and rich experience of conducting research among tribal societies of Bihar as well as of Gujarat. He has written several books and reports on tribals and published more than 30 papers on different aspects of tribal life and culture as well as their developmental problems.

**K.M. Kulkarni** (*b.* 1949) is Reader in Geography, Gujarat University, Ahmedabad. His main interests are urban and regional studies. He has Published more than 30 research papers in national and international journals and is the author of *Urban Structure and Interaction* (Concept, 1981), *Geography of Crowding and Human Response* (Concept, 1984) and *Geographical Patterns of Social Well-being in Gujarat* (Concept, 1989).

# FOREST AND TRIBAL LIFE

## [Study of a Micro-Region]

SOCIO-CULTURAL TRAITS SUSTAINING TRIBAL ECOLOGY
A CASE STUDY OF DANTA TALUKA,
BANASKANTHA DISTRICT, NORTH GUJARAT

Rohit Shukla
Ambubhai T. Desai
A.B. Vora
R.B. Lal
K.M. Kulkarni

CONCEPT PUBLISHING COMPANY PVT. LTD.
NEW DELHI-110059

This study was sponsored by The Development of Environment and Forest, Government of India.

**ISBN : 978-81-7022-277-4**

Edition 2018

*Published and Printed by*

**Concept Publishing Company Pvt. Ltd.**
Since 1974
A/15-16, Commercial Block, Mohan Garden,
New Delhi-110059 (INDIA)
*T* : +91 11 25351460, +91 11 25351794
*E* : publishing@conceptpub.com, *W* : www.conceptpub.com

**Cataloging in Publication Data**--Courtesy: D.K. Agencies (P) Ltd. <docinfo@dkagencies.com>

**Śukla, Rohita,** 1939- **author.**

Forest and tribal life : study of a micro-region : socio-cultural traits sustaining tribal ecology, a case study of Danta Taluka, Banaskantha District, north Gujarat / Rohit Shukla, Ambubhai T. Desai, A.B. Vora, R.B. Lal, K.M. Kulkarni.

pages cm

Reprint. Originally published: 1990.
Includes bibliographical references and index.
ISBN 9788170222774 (hardback)

1. Nature--Effect of human beings on--India--Danta (Taluka) 2. Forest ecology--India--Danta (Taluka) 3. Material culture--India--Danta (Taluka) 4. Subsistence economy--India--Danta (Taluka) 5. Danta (India : Taluka)--Social life and customs. I. Desai, Ambubhai T., 1932- author. II. Vora, A. B., 1933- author. III. Lal, Rash Bihari, 1935- author. IV. Kulkarni, K. M. (Krishnamurthy Mahadevrao), 1949- author. V. Sardar Patel Institute of Economic and Social Research. VI. Title.

LCC GF662.D37S85 2018 | DDC 304.28095475  23

# CONTENTS

# LIST OF TABLES

# APPENDIX TABLES

# LIST OF FIGURES & PHOTOGRAPHS

FIGURES



PHOTOGRAPHS

# PREFACE

TRIBALS LIVE in the eastern hilly region of the State of Gujarat. Anthropologically they are not entirely homogeneous. The tribals are economically and socially far backward than other social groups. Their backwardness is a result of a number of factors.

Socially they are out of the main stream of life. Because of very low rate of literacy, underdeveloped economy, peculiar nature and form of worship, customs and traditions, they have remained away from the general run of life. Besides, their secluded existence is reinforced by hilly and forested surroundings.

Since the tribals were living with the forests, their life style is full of customs and traditions where forests play a significant role. Forest products are used by them in a variety of ways, e.g., as material for housing, agricultural implements, transport, fuel, medicine, etc. Forests also provide them hunting ground for game. Collection of minor forest products, like, honey, lac, fruits, flowers, gums, resins and various ingredients of Ayurvedic system of medicine etc. It also provides good deal of gainful employment to the forest dwellers.

Fuelwood is also an important forest resource. But as more and more trees were felled, the forest became less and less dense. With decreasing forest wealth, income from other forest-based sources also decreased. As a result, still larger number of trees were cut to maintain the same economic level of the household. Two other factors also added to the deepening of this crisis.

Rapidly increasing population created a pressure on the forests. This initially led to an increase in the land under agriculture. When increasing human population was accompanied by increasing livestock also, the pressure on forest resources became too heavy. Browsing and grazing of livestock affected natural re-generation. The tribals and other communities, owning herds, chopped the browsable species for leaf fodder while heavy hoofed animals compacted soil; all these made re-generation of forest still more difficult.

Forests felt the economic pressure because of other two reasons as well. Since tribal community was away from the main stream, their outmigration in search of better economic opportunities was minimal. The pressure of increasing population had to be borne by a land-based economic activity. In this situation, secondly, the problem of slower growth rate in the yield rates of crop agriculture also became detrimental to forests. If the tribals had been able to achieve a better growth rate of agriculture along with better marketing facility, their income levels could have been higher enough and their dependence on forests could have been lesser. The forests, as common property, were privatised because of the continuation of almost exclusive reliance on land-based activities.

As forests dwindled, the nutrituon of tribal diet also suffered because of loss of game. This loss also had to be compensated by forests - if not exclusively, at least partialy. All these factors combined to create excessive pressure on forests. Once the pressure was felt and there was no countervailing measure to decrease it, the forces behind the pressure bacame self-reinforcing.

Our study shows that the tribals have a very close affinity with the forests. They are dependent on them not only for their economic requirements, but more importantly, they have a strong cultural link with the forests. Though, indeed, the tribal development policy of the government does better than considering them museum pieces, the whole approach of their economic development can not be sufficiently satisfying without forest development. The policy of forest development however shall have to be more broadly specified and carefully developed.

This pilot study aims at looking into the socio-cultural traits amongst the tribals which sustain the eco-system at the level of this micro-region. Since a more detailed study would be required for a comprehensive understanding, in this study we have considered the relevant issues from the angles of food and housing only.

The study was entrusted to us by the Department of Environment, Government of India. In order to capture various dimensions of the tribal life, we formed an inter-disciplinary and inter-institutional team.

The team consisted of the following:

(1) Prof. Rohit Shukla, Economics
(Project Co-ordinator)
Professor of Economics,

Sardar Patel Institute of Economic and Social Research.

(2) Prof. Ambubhai T Desai, Geography
Pro-Vice Chancellor,
Gujarat University.

(3) Prof. A B Vora, Botany
Professor and Head, Botany Department
Gujarat University.

(4) Dr. R B Lal, Social Anthropology
Tribal Research Centre,
Gujarat Vidyapeeth.

(5) Dr. K M Kulkarni, Geography
Geography Department, Gujarat University.

We are grateful to the Department of Environment, Government of India, for entrusting this pilot study to us. Our thanks are due to an anonymous referee who has gone through the draft report and offered us valuable comments and suggestions.

We are thankful to Shri Dhiren Avashia, Co-ordinator, EMRC, Gujarat University for help in arranging for photography and Shri. Makbool Chavda of EMRC for taking the photographs.

Our thanks are also due to Dr. P G Pathak for helping us in arrangements for putting this report on the Word Processor, at times sparing his valuable time and working at the Word Processor himself.

We are also grateful to the authorities of Banaskantha district and Danta taluka for valuable comments and background information. Our thanks are due to the local authorities at the village level for providing necessary help. We are indeed grateful to the local people who agreed to respond to our detailed inquiry into their personal affairs. But for their willingness to co-operate, no such study could have been possible.

Rohit Shukla
Ambubhai T Desai
A B Vora
R B Lal
K M Kulkarni

# GLOSSARY - I

Adobe - hand made flat tiles, used to cover roof; made locally
Ambli - Tamarind
Ambo - a mango tree
Athir - horizontal beams at a head height in the room; used for storage purpose
Ayurved - indegenous system of medicine
Bajri - pearl millet
Bali - a small broom used for collecting flour from the hand-flour mill (Ghanti)
Bapota - land inherited from one's own father
Bhajan - devotional song
Bidi - indegenous cigarettes
Bor - a locally available fruit - *Ziziphus spp.*
Bunti - a coarse millet
Chaku - a small knife
Chhari - a hunter's knife
Chino - gram
Choel - root-bark of Khakhara tree, used to make ropes and cords
Chulo - a mud oven
Daglo - a wooden platform raised in the courtyard supported by wooden posts and used for stacking hay, drying grains, etc.
Datan - a tooth-brush, usually a twig of finger thickness of baval (*Acacia nilotica*) or limdo (*Azadirachta indica*)
Datru (Datardu) - sickle - a farm implement
Deshi - indegenous - local
Dhariyu - a sharp and long iron blade (10 to 12 inches long) mounted on bamboo (about 5 feet long), used for

| | |
|---|---|
| | chopping small branches etc., also occassionally used as a weapon. |
| Dhol | - a drum, eliptical in shape |
| Dhule-na-pat | - a tribal god |
| Dholi musli | - local vegetation collected as an MFP, believed to be aphrodesia, whitish in colour. |
| Dhotli | - a loin cloth wrapped around waist |
| Doli | - mahuda (*Madhuca indica*) seed |
| ek sali | - (lit.) of one yearly basis, usually land taken or lease (mostly from the forest department) on one yearly basis |
| Ghanti | - a pair of grinding stones |
| Ghar | - a house |
| Ghara land | - Plain land |
| Ghee | - purified butter |
| Gofan | - a long string with a wide leather piece at the centre to hold a small stone, used to drive away birds from the ripened fields |
| Gram-sevak | - village level extension worker (lit.) village servant |
| Gugal | - an MFP, a gum like exude from *Comifera wightli*, used for fragrant smoke in temples or during religious ceremonies |
| Har | - a plough |
| Jav | - barley |
| Kali musli | - same as 'dholi musli' but darkish in colour |
| Karab | - a farm implement - leveller |
| Katha | - a powder extracted from khair (*Acacia catechue*) tree, used in pan (beetle leaf) |
| Kathrot | - a utensil, made from brass also from wood, a little larger than 'thali' (plate) |
| Khajuri | - a date palm tree |
| Khatla | - same as charpai, sleeping cots, of various sizes (Khatlo-Khatli denoted by khatli - small size, khatlo - big size) |
| Khatli | - also a frame, raised for the purpose of storage, used on 'Athir' |
| Kho | - a wooden churner for making butter and butter milk |
| Kodra | - a coarse millet |
| Kosh | - a water moat |

Kudi - a musical instrument made from chips of bamboo
Kuhadi - axe, used to cut wood
Lakdi - a stick generally of bamboo and about five feet long
Lota - a water jug
Mador - central and long beam in the house
Makai - maize
Matla - a pitcher
Mehre - a farm implement
Mocho - same as khatla
Morli - flute
Nadi - a river, a stream
Nagara - a pair of small drums, circular in shape
Padiya-patrala - leaf cup and plates (respectively), usually made from khakhara leaves
Panch - a group of village elders (lit.) a group of five persons
Pavti, rahat - a water wheel, persian wheel, the former is worked by human labour and the latter by animal labour
Pathra land - stony land or rocky land
Paithar - verandah
Pat - main beam in the house
Piyat - irrigated (un-irrigated) (bin-piyat)
Pavala - a water cup (glass)
Police patel - village head man
Pucca - masonry construction
Ramdeo pir - a saint, having followings in Muslims as well as Hindus
Rampuri chaku - a strong, big and sharp knife used as a weapon
Rap - a farm implement
Samar - a farm implement, leveller
Saran method - method of gravitational flow; used for irrigating fields through water collected at a height
Shamans - tribal men of diognosis and healing
Shankhali - conch, used as a musical instrument
Shikar - hunting
Supda - used for winnowing and separating grains from chaff, usually made from bamboo chips
Tali, manjira - small symbal made from brass
Talwar - a sword

| | |
|---|---|
| Tawa | - a round iron disc used for baking bread |
| Temro, tamburs | - a stringed musical instrument |
| Thali | - plate |
| Thamba | - pillars which support 'Daglo' |
| Thaliyo | - a circular wooden structure on which 'Ghanti' is mounted; used to collect flour |
| Tir-kamtha | - an arrow and a bow |
| Tirpaya | - wooden poles, used to support 'Athir' |
| Trifala | - contains three ayarvedic fruits, heda, baheda and ambala, an ayurvedic medicine. The fruits are collected as MFP |
| Topla | - a basket |
| Tur | - pulse |
| Urad | - pulse |
| Vahal-vahali | - flutes of big and small sizes |

# GLOSSARY - II

(A) Agricultural Crops:

| Srl. No. | Botanical Name | Local Name |
|---|---|---|
| 1. | Avena sterilis | Oat |
| 2. | Brassica juncea | Rayado |
| 3. | Cajanus cajan | Tuver |
| 4. | Chenopodium album | Chil-ni-bhaji |
| 5. | Cicer arietinum | Chana |
| 6. | Echinochloa frumentacea | Banti |
| 7. | Eleusine corcana | Nagli |
| 8. | Hordeum vulgare | Jav, Sattu |
| 9. | Paspalum scrobiculatum | Kodra |
| 10. | Pennisetum typhoides | Bajri |
| 11. | Sesamum orientale | Tal |
| 12. | Vigna angularis | Adad |
| 13. | Zea mays | Makai |

Note: Crops under serial nos. 1 and 7 to 11 are also used as fodder crops.

(B) Other Species

Note: Original identity of the following species is not established. Hence only local names are mentioned.

1. Chino
2. Golar
3. Halar
4. Maju
5. Ponch
6. Sabai grass
7. Sajija
8. Sahoh
9. Saiti
10. Sava
11. Savan

# 1

# INTRODUCTION

THERE IS a growing concern among the technocrats, bureaucrats and politicians to protect and improve the quality of environmental resources, such as, air, water, soil, vegetation and minerals, through various measures. Such steps become absolutely necessary in the countries where advanced level of institutional and technological set-up exists. The environmental conditions in the majority of the Third World countries have started becoming grave and more so in the pockets of industrial, urbanised and dense rural areas. These are the areas of intense resource exploitation. Some of the tribal areas and remote rural areas in the Third World countries have better environmental quality and balance, mainly because of some prevailing religious beliefs and non-availability of modern technological means. However, one finds the impact of urbanisation making inroads in the tribal environment to the extent of resource utilisation and influencing the environmental conditions.

The study of socio-cultural traits sustaining eco-system in a micro-region in North Gujarat was entrusted to the Sardar Patel Institute of Economic and Social Research in collaboration with the Gujarat University and Gujarat Vidyapeeth by the Department of Environment of the Government of India. Considering the availability of funds and time it was thought desirable to study only two major manifestations, viz., food and housing, in this pilot study. The present study aims at enquiring into socio-cultural traits of tribals in sustaining their eco-system from the angle of requirements regarding food and housing.

A production system in any micro-region is based on its environmental conditions and resource base in general. Cropping pattern, for example, depends on surface configuration of soil, water and conditions of sunshine. Flora and Fauna of any region can exist, survive and continue to thrive only if the equilibrium of an eco-system is left undisturbed. But, in the present day context the imbalance in the eco-system has become alarming in many parts of the world. Depletion of forests has not only created a crisis of fuelwood, timber and industrial raw materials but also a variety of fundamental problems like erosion of soil, siltation of rivers, reservoirs and tanks, loss of wild life and birds, etc. All these culminate in the dislocation of life styles and culture of tribals as their life style is governed by the eco-system of a region.

The present field of enquiry, viz., the impact of environment on food and housing, is an important area of study. The tribal households living in backward areas are known to shun markets. They satisfy their necessities of these two economic goods by using freely available commodities. Supply of such commodities is becoming scarcer with increasing population pressure of the tribals and increasing road and other facilities resulting in opening up of the areas. Their felt needs are, however, met from subsistence farmimg.

In non-market situations, tribals are found to rely on general environment for their sustenance. Forest produce, like, bomboo has many expressions as farm or non-farm implements, housing material, etc. A moot point arises here also: Can the use of physical environment along with human environment lead to modernisation with the help of improvements in technology?

People living in such areas cannot remain disinterested regarding their own environment as their life style and, at times, existence is dependent on it. A question can legitimately be asked : Do people, living in such areas, realise the full significance of forests in particular and environment in general? If so what measures are taken by the society, in general, to maintain and develop necessary forest and other resources?

Since forest and other environmental aspects are matters neither of direct nor of immediate concern for individuals, its importance is to be realised by the group and social pattern of behaviour.

The environment and, in particular, the forest wealth of the country have been deteriorating at an alarming rate. The situation is more or less equally bad or even worse at the State level. Though the government has undertaken the activity of growing trees, its success depends on the acceptance of such programmes by the people. People's acceptance, again, partly depends on their traditions, customs and culture. It would be very interesting to find out such cultural traits which could be then reinforced to derive a better support for environment.

Forest produce is used by tribals in a number of ways. So far as food and diet are concerned the tribals are known to consume non-traditional diets, particularly, during drought conditions. Tribals' relationship with forests encompasses a wide spectrum of life including medicines, musical instruments, housing material, agricultural implements, etc.

Approximately 14 per cent of population of the State is tribal. There are many tribal groups like Bhil, Koli, Kotwalia, Dhodia, Nayak, Nayakda, etc., inhabiting the eastern fringe of the State which is an undulating and hilly terrain and is covered with sparse forests. However, these forest resources are also depleting rapidly. Since the inception of the State in 1960 to present day, 1.5 lakh hectares (13 per cent) of forests are lost. The State is left with only 19.6 lakh hectares of forests. This is 10 per cent of the total geographical area of the State. Only 51 per cent of this forest area is economically productive. Since the tribal life depends on the diversity of primeval forest its symbiosis with ambient ecology needs to be used for ecological conservation.

## Objectives

This research project aims at identifying customs, traditions, cultural traits and habits which tend to preserve environment and use natural and living resources on a sustainable basis with a view to looking into the impact of environment on food and housing. As such it aims at collecting and analysing data in an integrated fashion from multi-disciplinary angle. This pilot project has the following objectives:

(a) Geographical survey of environmental resources pertaining to food and housing such as tree crops, agricultural crops, root crops and building materials (in relation to topography, geography, geology, climate, economic condition and cultural requirement).

(b) Study of living resources by species of vegetation and wild life in relation to food and housing.

(c) Study of pattern of resource use in :

(i) Production sectors like agriculture, forestry, animal husbandry and

(ii) Consumption sectors like food and housing.

(d) Study of social and anthropological traits, habits, traditions, skills, etc., which emphasise the use of resources in a sustainable way in this regard.

(e) Study of economic causes either reinforcing such cultural traits or damaging them in light of increasing modernisations caused by economic compulsion.

(f) To draw plans for development of appropriate methodology which could be adopted for broad-based studies in future.

## Methodology

Considering the multi-disciplinary nature of the study, a team, consisting of five experts belonging to four different disciplines, was formed. The disciplines encompassed are: Anthropology, Botany, Economics and Geography. These experts are working in different institutions and hence this is an inter-institutional effort as well.

In order to evolve a cohesive approach to the project, integrate the strands of ideas and experience and cast the enquiry into a unified study, continuous interaction of the experts was required. Hence, the team was served by one co-ordinator who also arranged for smooth functioning of the project.

For the purpose of this pilot study Danta taluka of Banaskantha district in North Gujarat was purposively selected. From this taluka a total of four villages were selected. The selection of villages was based on three criteria which emerged from the objectives of the study. These were: (a) proximity or otherwise of road, (b) size of village population and (c) micro-geographical differences (in topography and forest cover). The matrix of criteria in the sample space led to identification of four villages which were as follows:

| | Sample characteristics | Name of villages and Area | |
|---|---|---|---|
| (i) | Connected by road and small (CS) | Pansa | Hilly Area |
| (ii) | Connected by road and large (CL) | Sembalpani | " |
| (iii) | Not connected by road and small (NCS) | Mahuda | Plain Area |
| (iv) | Not connected by road and large (NCL) | Sandhosi | " |

While selecting these villages discussions were held with the officials of ITDP, Banaskantha, and officials of taluka panchayat, Danta. Villages suggested by these two sets were personally visited by the whole team of experts and the details regarding village size and road connection and also the differences in the micro-geographical conditions were personally checked.

At the final stage of selecting respondent households, criterion of size proportion was adopted. The information of land ownership, as recorded in these village panchayats, was used to classify land ownership into four land-size, (LS) classes. These LS classes were:

(a) 0.01 to 1.00 ha,
(b) 1.01 to 2.00 ha,
(c) 2.01 to 4.00 ha and
(d) 4.01 to above ha.

All households of each sample village were arranged into these four classes. The proportion of households belonging to each of these LS categories at the level of each village was calculated. A total of 20 per cent of households was selected as sample; maintaining the village level proportionally and using a random number table. An additional replacement list of households was also prepared in case a selected household turned out to be non-available or non-co-operative. The final sampling outcome is shown in Table 1.1.

It is interesting to note (Table 1.2) that the pattern of land ownership in case of tribals is remarkably less skewed as compared to the State level pattern. The first two classes of land ownership, in case of tribals, form 60.3 percentage of farmers while in case of the State this proportion is 43 per cent. Medium size farmers, in case of the tribal area, forms nearly 24 per cent as compared to 30 per cent in case of Gujarat. In case of tribals, very few farmers are owning more than 5.00 ha of land. Their proportion of less than seven per cent is in sharp contrast to 27 per cent in case of Gujarat State.

TABLE 1.1: **Sample Villages and LS Class-wise Size of Sample Drawn**

| *Sr. No.* | *Village* | *Village Category* | *LS Class* | *No. of Sample households* | *Villagewise Proportion (in %)* |
|---|---|---|---|---|---|
| 1 | 2 | 3 | 4 | 5 | 6 |
| 1. | Pansa | C S | (a) 0.01 to 1.00 | 10 | 50 |
| | | | (b) 1.01 to 2.00 | 7 | 35 |
| | | | (c) 2.01 to 4.00 | 3 | 15 |
| | | | (d) 4.01 + | - | - |
| | | | (e) Others | nil | - |
| | | | Total | 20 | 100 |
| 2. | Sembalpani | C L | (a) 0.01 to 1.00 | 1 | 5 |
| | | | (b) 1.01 to 2.00 | 3 | 15 |
| | | | (c) 2.01 to 4.00 | 1 | 5 |
| | | | (d) 4.01 + | 1 | 5 |
| | | | (e) Others | 14 | 70 |
| | | | Total | 20 | 100 |
| 3. | Mahuda | NCS | (a) 0.01 to 1.00 | 1 | 20 |
| | | | (b) 1.01 to 2.00 | 1 | 20 |
| | | | (c) 2.01 to 4.00 | 2 | 40 |
| | | | (d) 4.01 + | 1 | 20 |
| | | | (e) Others | nil | - |
| | | | Total | 5 | 100 |
| 4. | Sandhosi | NCL | (a) 0.01 to 1.00 | 11 | 39.3 |
| | | | (b) 1.01 to 2.00 | 10 | 35.7 |
| | | | (c) 2.01 to 4.00 | 4 | 14.3 |
| | | | (d) 4.01 + | 3 | 10.7 |
| | | | (e) Others | nil | 0.0 |
| | | | Total | 28 | 100.0 |

Thus for each LS class the sampling outcome works out to a distribution which is shown in table 1.2.

TABLE 1.2: **L S Class-wise distribution of Sample Households**

| *Sl. No.* | *L S Category* | *No. of Sample Households* | *Percentege of sample house-holds to total* | *State level distribution of L S Classes* |
|---|---|---|---|---|
| 1. | (a) 0.01 to 1.00 | 23 | 31.5 | 24 |
| 2. | (b) 1.01 to 2.00 | 21 | 28.8 | 19 |
| 3. | (c) 2.01 to 4.00 | 10 | 23.7 | 30 ** |
| 4. | (d) 4.01 and above | 5 | 6.8 | 27 ** |
| 5. | (e) Others | 14 | 19.2 | - |
| | Total | 73 | 100.00 | 100.00 |

* Computed from agricultural census 1976-77 (unpublished) Gandhinagar : Revenue Dept. (GOG).

** These two categories are differently classified as 2.01 to 5.00 ha. and 5.01 and above. Hence these two do not become comparable.

# 2

# SALIENT FEATURES OF THE AREA OF STUDY

## Location

DANTA TALUKA, one of the eleven talukas of Banaskantha district, shares its boundry with Sabarkantha district on the east and Rajasthan State on the north. It was found suitable for the purposes of carrying out this pilot study. The four sample villages, namely, Pansa, Sandhosi, Sembalpani and Mahuda were selected out of the total 186 villages of the taluka in such a way that these villages represented different micro-geographical environments i.e., (1) relatively rugged topography (with high average altitude) covered with moderately dense vegetation and (2) relatively low altitude with large tracts of arable land and scanty scrubland. It is widely assumed and established with findings that such contrasting micro-geographical environments influence the socio-cultural traits of tribal communities in a significant way resulting into a contrasting pattern.

## General background

The grand chain of Aravalli mountains, on the north-east of Gujarat, forms a line running north-east and south-east right from Delhi to the plains of Gujarat. The Aravalli ranges which bound Gujarat on the north and the east and which projects numerous branches into the nearest parts of the State are steep, craggy and difficult to reach. In the shoulders of the hills and the valleys, which intervene between the spurs, the villages of Danta taluka are situated. Geologically it is considered to be the oldest mountain system in India - millions of years older than Himalayas.

The taluka has the oldest rock formations found in the district which belong to the pre-cambrian age (more than 3,500 million years ago). These are represented by Ajabgarh group of meta-sediments

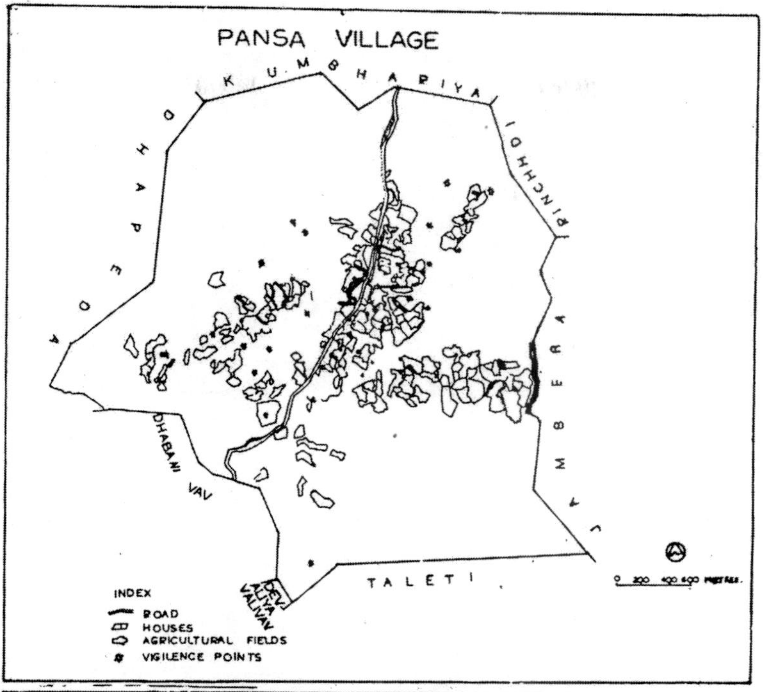
PANSA VILLAGE
KUMBHARIYA
PINCHHDI
JAMBERA
TALETI
DEV ALIYA VALIVAV
DHABANI VAV
ADEPAHD
0 200 400 600 METRES.
INDEX
ROAD
HOUSES
AGRICULTURAL FIELDS
VIGILENCE POINTS

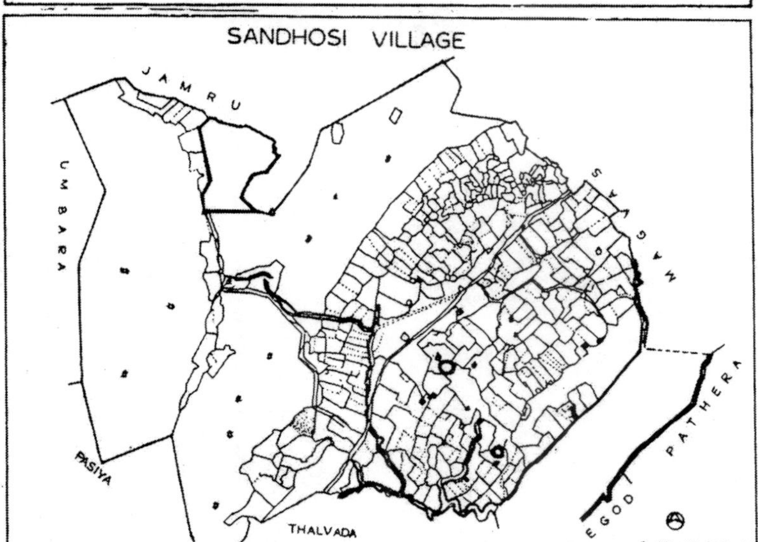
SANDHOSI VILLAGE
JAMRU
UMBARA
SAGAM
PATHERA
BEGOD
THALVADA
PASIYA
INDEX
DRY STREAM
HOUSES
AGRICULTURAL FIELDS
VIGILENCE POINTS
ROAD

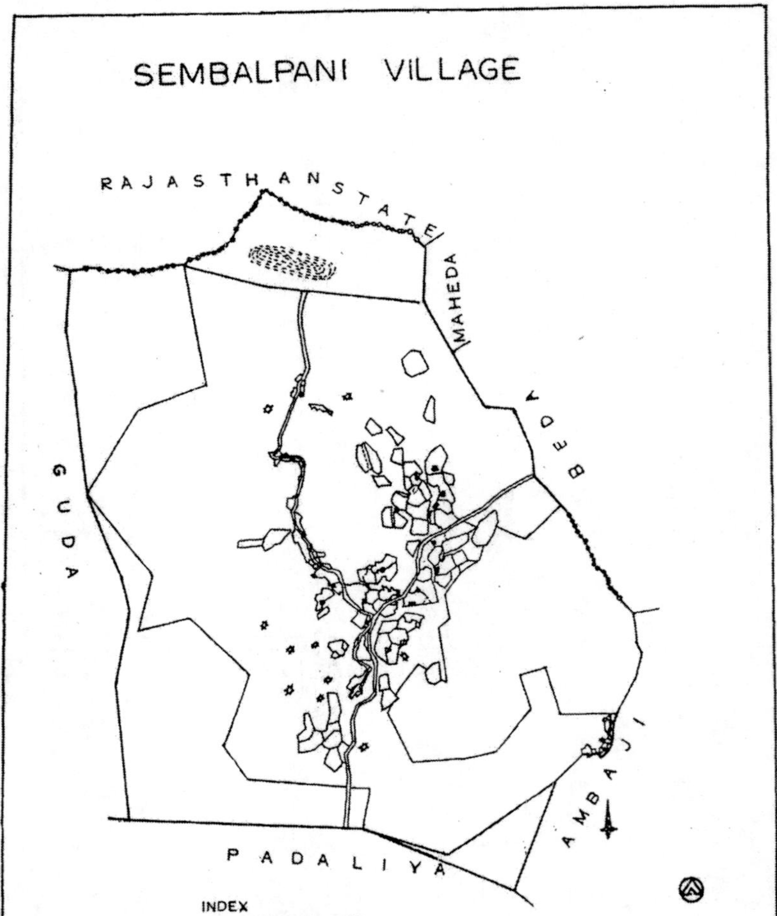
SEMBALPANI VILLAGE
RAJASTHAN STATE
MAHEDA
BEDA
GUDA
AMBAJI
PADALIYA
INDEX
DRY STREAM BED
HOUSES
AGRICULTURAL FIELDS
VIGILENCE POINTS
0 200 400 600 METRE

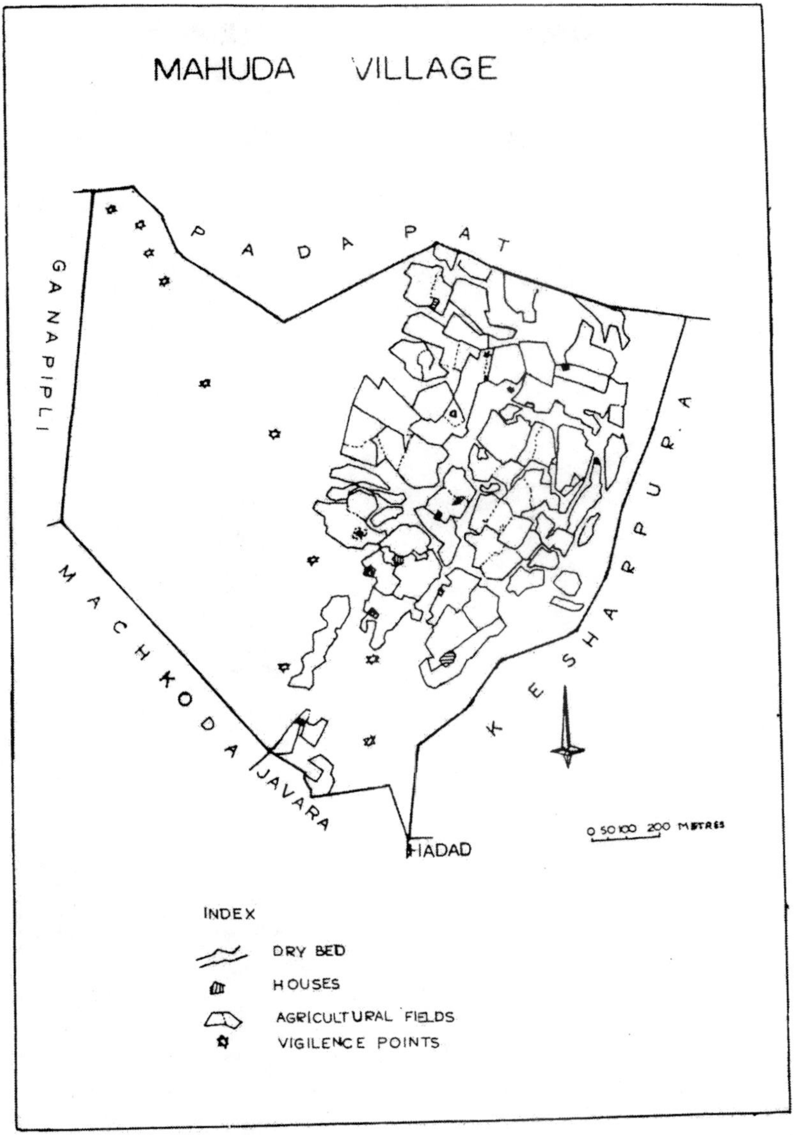
MAHUDA VILLAGE
PADAPAT
GANAPIPLI
MACHKODA
JAVARA
HADAD
KESHARPURA
0 50 100 200 METRES
INDEX
DRY BED
HOUSES
AGRICULTURAL FIELDS
VIGILENCE POINTS

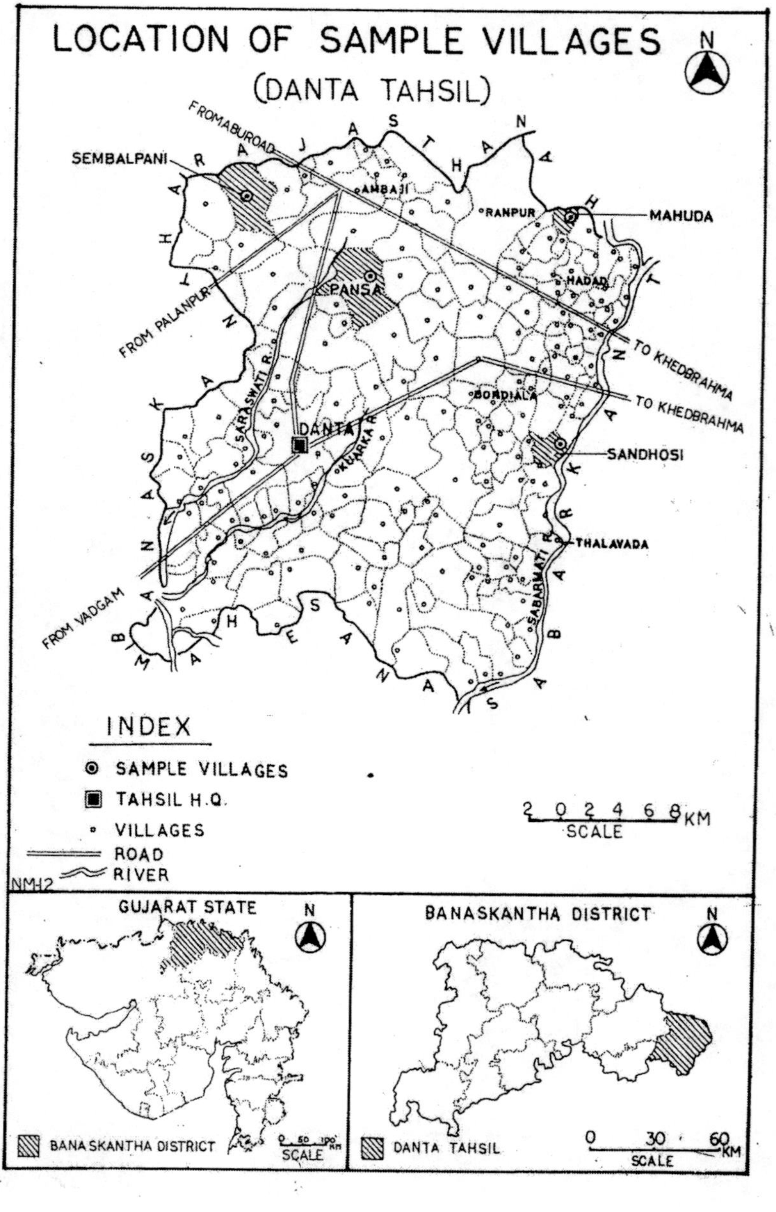
LOCATION OF SAMPLE VILLAGES
(DANTA TAHSIL)
N
RAJASTHAN
FROM ABUROAD
SEMBALPANI
AMBAJI
RANPUR
MAHUDA
HADAD
PANSA
FROM PALANPUR
TO KHEDBRAHMA
TO KHEDBRAHMA
BORDIALA
SARASWATI R.
DANTA
KURKA R.
SANDHOSI
THALAVADA
SABARMATI R.
BANASKANTHA
SABARKANTHA
MEHSANA
FROM VADGAM
INDEX
SAMPLE VILLAGES
TAHSIL H.Q.
VILLAGES
ROAD
RIVER
2 0 2 4 6 8 KM
SCALE
NMI2
GUJARAT STATE
N
BANASKANTHA DISTRICT
0 50 100 KM
SCALE
BANASKANTHA DISTRICT
N
DANTA TAHSIL
0 30 60 KM
SCALE

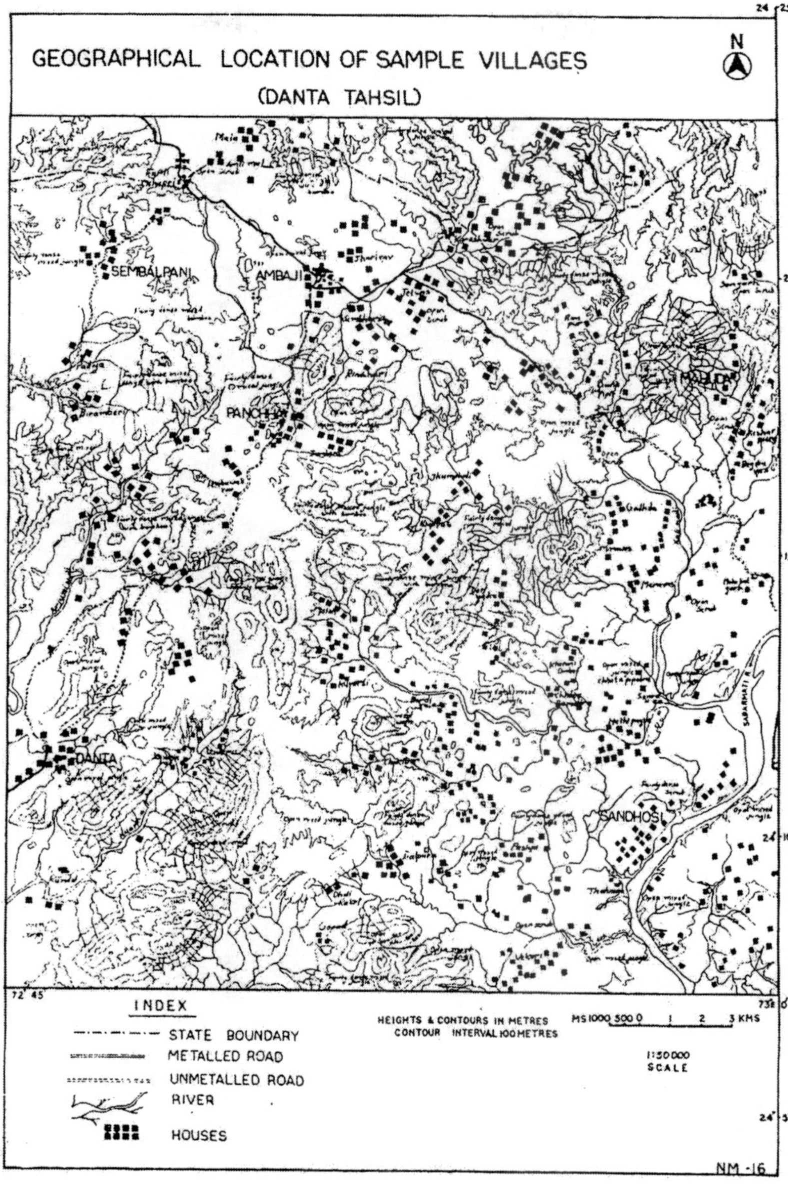
GEOGRAPHICAL LOCATION OF SAMPLE VILLAGES
(DANTA TAHSIL)
N
SEMBALPANI
AMBAJI
PANCHHA
DANTA
SANDHOSI
SABARMATI R.
INDEX
STATE BOUNDARY
METALLED ROAD
UNMETALLED ROAD
RIVER
HOUSES
HEIGHTS & CONTOURS IN METRES
CONTOUR INTERVAL 100 METRES
1:50000
SCALE
3 KMS
NM-16

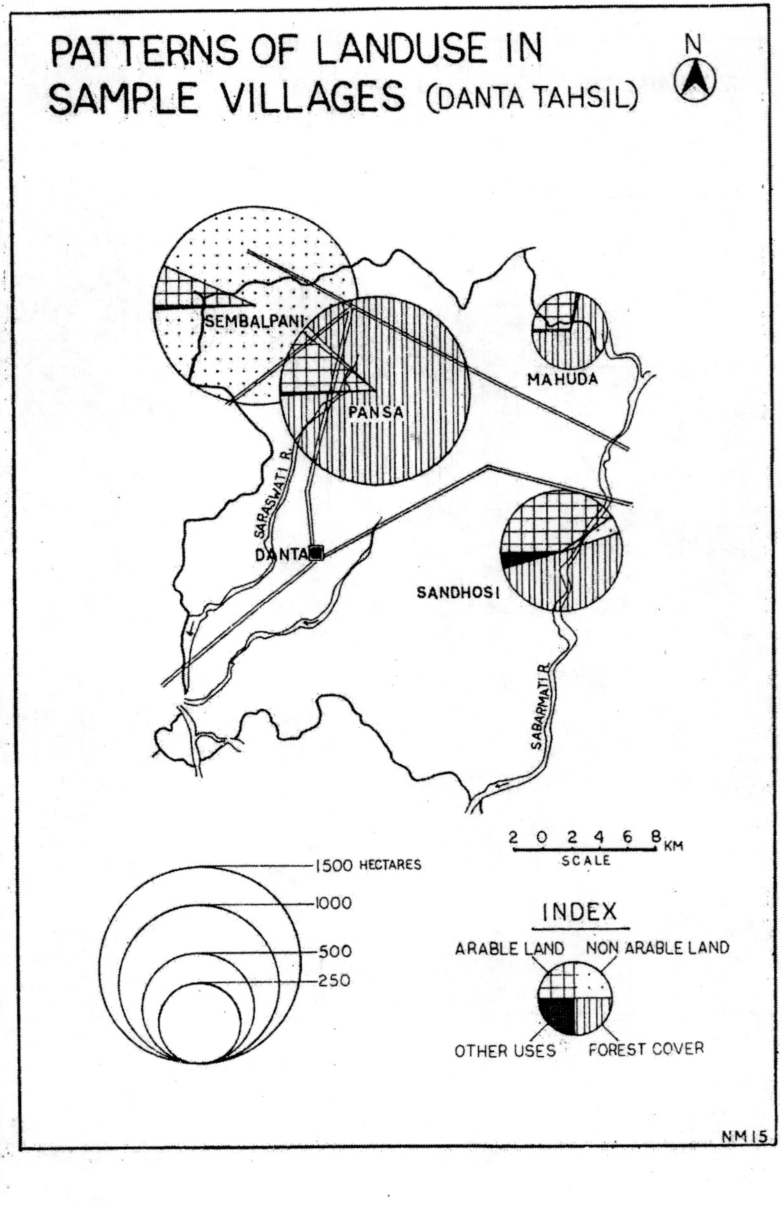
PATTERNS OF LANDUSE IN
SAMPLE VILLAGES (DANTA TAHSIL)
N
SEMBALPANI
PANSA
MAHUDA
SARASWATI R.
DANTA
SANDHOSI
SABARMATI R.
2 0 2 4 6 8 KM
SCALE
1500 HECTARES
1000
500
250
INDEX
ARABLE LAND
NON ARABLE LAND
OTHER USES
FOREST COVER
NM15

which include calcareous rocks (like marble and calogneiss), argillaceous rocks (like phyllite and mica schists) and arenaceous rocks, (like quartzite, quartz schists, etc.). Subsequent to these depositions there were three phases of igneous activity which have been metamorphosed.

Ambaji base metal project is located at Ambaji in Danta taluka. This includes the processing of multi-mineral ore talc-schist rock with 13.50 per cent total metal content having a share of 5.5 per cent lead, six per cent zinc and two per cent copper. There are several deposits of high grade limestone in the taluka and based on it a cement factory has been established near village Mahuda (Radhakrishna Cement Factory). Around Ambaji, some of the best quality marble occurs which are of both white and greenish varieties. These reserves offer ample opportunities to make stonewares of domestic, artistic and religious value. Other minerals include wollastonite (Ghoda village of Danta taluka) and calcite (Path-Jitpur and Ghantodi villages) in minor quantities. These mineral resources may provide good means of livelihood for the tribal communities provided the State government works out various schemes of mineral-based development including quarrying activities.

Granite reposing is found in a variety of angle (the general dip is to the east) on massive compact, dark blue slate, the latter rarely appearing much above the surface or base of the super incumbent granite. It is believed that "....... the Aravallis are but the depressed and degraded relic of a far more prominent mountain system, which stood in paleaozoic times on the edge of Rajputana".[1] The geological formations of these hills belong to azoic and igneous group. The internal valleys abound in variegated quartz and variety of schistous slate of every hue. The Aravalli and its subordinate hills are rich in both mineral and metallic products. Marble, limestone, bauxite and rock for stone quarry are available in the taluka. Danta taluka is the largest producer of marble and has the State's largest known deposits of marble.

The Geological Survey of India has also reported deposits of copper. Copper mining activities have been started under the aegis of the Gujarat Mineral Development Corporation (GMDC). However, ochre and limestones among the major minerals and gravel and kankar among the minor ones are commercially worked in the taluka. A cement factory has been established in the region to utilise these raw materials. It also has commercially workable deposits of bentonite,

Fulter's earth, calcite, felspar, sandstone, wollastonites and base metals of zinc, lead and copper.

The southern part of the Aravalli range is mostly a network of forest clad hills enclosing well-watered valleys and table land. The southern range of the Aravalli may be considered as an extension of the mountainous region of Pali and Udaipur districts in Rajasthan, while its branches extend up to Sabarkantha district of Gujarat. In Gujarat this range cuts across the north-east of Banaskantha and Sabarkantha districts. Thus, the entire Danta taluka is marked by the hill ranges of Aravalli. The steep and craggy hills of pink or grey granites do not exceed about 700 metres in height in Danta taluka. Even the highest peak, Gurushikhar on Mt. Abu, is 1,722 metres high. The whole region is very picturesque and presents a beautiful high land scenery. Danta is a land of thousand hills although possessing no peaks or hills of special interest. This taluka is bounded in north by Rajasthan State, in the south by Mehsana and Sabarkantha districts, in the east by Rajasthan State and Sabarkantha district and in the west by the Palanpur and Vadgam talukas of the Banaskantha district.

Physiographically the district of Banaskantha is divided into three micro-regions. They are hilly, rugged topography in the east, the piedmont zone and the plain area in the west. The hilly region in the east has a high relief and the rugged terrain is covered with natural vegetation. Danta taluka falls under hilly region which extends to cover parts of the adjacent talukas, namely, Dhanera, Palanpur and Vadgam. The four selected sample villages of Danta taluka are situated approximately between 24°10′ N and 24°20′ N latitude and 72°45′ E and 73°0′ E longitude. The mean sea-level (MSL) of the area is about 400-500 metres with a number of isolated hilly peaks ranging from 700 to 860 metres. These isolated hillocks are part of the Aravalli[2] hill ranges which are covered with fairly dense mixed jungle with bamboo interspersed with open mixed jungle. There are number of gullies of small dry streams in the study region. The Teliya Nadi (stream) which flows west of Gabbar in NNW direction takes its origin in the hilly area, east of Pansa. The Arjun Nadi which originates west of Pansa flows in SSW direction. The area around Sembalpani also forms part of the catchment area of the Teliya Nadi. By and large the area on the east of Ambaji is a catchment area of the Kidi Nadi, having undulating topography with dense mixed jungle, except around Mahuda (NCS) where it gives rise to open scrubland. Hadad is a relatively larger settlement located 5 kms. south of Mahuda, on the trijunction of State highway and major District Road.

The important economic activities include agriculture and animal husbandry as the micro-region provides large grazing land and ample fodder. Sandhosi, another sample village situated on the bank of the Sabarmati river, has a wide stretch of arable land including the large isolated pockets of dense scrubland. The wide riverbed of the Sabarmati shelters thin blade of water flow. The MSL around Sandhosi (NCL) village is about 250 metres and like Mahuda village here also the agricultural and animal husbandry activities are important. Sample villages of hilly, rugged topography with fairly dense jungle are located at an average altitude of 430 metres above MSL. Pansa, (CS, 480 metres), Sembalpani (CL, 380 metres) and the sample villages of plain, with arable and open scrub-land are located at an average altitude of 245 metres above MSL (Mahuda, NCS 290 metres, Sandhosi, NCL 200 metres).

The region experiences sub-tropical climate - cool and dry in winter and hot and slightly humid in summer season. The average annual rainfall of the region is 83.2 cms. (S.D. = 34.45 and C.V. = 42.6 per cent). the average monthly temperature during the year varies from 18°C in January to 35°C in May, with an average annual temperature of 27°C. The greater part of the taluka is covered by the tropical thorny forest with a core area having tropical dry mixed deciduous forest with bamboo. Fuel-wood, gum, resin, honey and other forest products are collected as sources of income and livelihood by the tribal inhabitants.

Danta taluka is famous throughout Gujarat and Rajasthan on account of having several places of pilgrimage for Hindus and Jains. The famous temple of Amba-Bhavani (Ambaji) lies embossomed among the hills of Arasoor, at the south-east termination of the Aravalli ranges in this taluka. Near Ambaji there is another famous place for pilgrimage at Koteshwar, where the temple of Lord Shiva (Koteshwar Mahadeva) is located. The small but translucent river Saraswati runs westward towards the Rann of Kutch, from this celebrated shrine of Koteshwar Mahadeva, in the marble hills of Arasoor. Also near Ambaji is a little village founded by Koombha Rana of Chittoor and called after his name, Koombharia. Here are located five magnificient Jain temples.

## NOTES

1. *The Imperial Gazetter of India*, Oxford (1967). 1.
2. 'Aravalli' literally means hills of strengh.

# 3

THE EARLIEST settlers, both rulers and ruled, in Danta taluka were the tribes known as Bhils. There are many evidences which establish the fact that before the Rajputs came in this area, the population in this Aravalli region consisted mainly of Bhils.

Bhils and Rajputs who were the two major ancestral stocks are generally believed to have contributed to the present tribal population of Danta taluka. One has been the indigenous population living in the Aravalli hills. The other has been the later immigrant in this area. They are the Rajput of the Indo-Aryan group. According to Sherring - "the Garasias are said to be descended from Chauhan Rajputs who were in the country before the Sisodia conquered Chittoor. They have lost most of their Rajput customs and are now a wild race, associating closely with the Bhils whose daughter they take in marriage and now they live apart from more civilised people".[1] It will not be true, however to say that the Garasias have descended from Chauhan Rajputs only. In fact the history of the region clearly and pointedly shows that nearly all sections of Rajputs had been inter-mingling with the Bhils. By inter-marriage with the Bhils, many of these Rajputs lost caste, only keeping the name of Rajput clans to which their forefathers belonged. Grierson has elucidated about the Garasias in following terms:[2] "It seems possible that the clan of Garasias arose from the fugitive Rajputs who joined the Bhils, temporarily or permanently, and had issues, legitimate or otherwise, by Bhil women and that the fruit of these union took, as distinguished mark, the clan name of the parent."[3]

The Aravalli mountain, the abode of the tribal people of this region, had been a scene of great historical turmoil and upheavals right from the period of the Rajput rulers to the early British rule. This happended on account of the large number of princely States in and around that region and frequent Mughal invasions on these princely States. Bloody feuds were the order of the day in those times. It has been narrated by Forbes: "At this time, the Gaikwad army used to come every three or four years and when the people of the villages heard of their approaching........ they caused the 'Trughyas' to beat their drums and raise a cry of 'Fly, Fly', the army is coming, upon which the people fled and, taking shelter among the hills, concealed themselves there with the Bhils".[4]

Thus, in an endeavour to gain peaceful life, the Rajput Jagirdars and Girasdars went to the length of adopting the way of life of Bhils, living in the remote hills and forest. It is not difficult to imagine that there was a constant influx of immigration on the part of the Rajputs to the hilly tracts, where the Bhils lived. It was the safest possible way for such fugitives to escape the bloody feuds. Those Rajput Jagirdars, who took refuge in the hills and who had lost their estate and hence had no Jagir, were prepared to identify themselves as Garasias as that was prestigious than to be called Bhils. The Rajputs who were absorbed in the then Bhil society kept their claim about their origin to Rajput caste and even stuck to their identified original clan name even though, in the course of time, they had identified themselves with the Bhils in the socio-cultural fashion.

This inter-marriage also helps in explaining the large number of groups and clans in the tribal society. C.S. Venkatachar traces Rajput blood in this situation also. "Forced by circumstances", he writes, "to make an alliance with the denizens of hills, the Rajputs did not hesitate to take women from tribal land and this was the reason of disintegration of the Bhils into various sections they own today."[5]

All these evidences suggest that the Garasias of Danta taluka have been distinctly referred to as an independent group irrespective of their past association with the Rajputs or Bhils. They were mainly concentrated,during the British period, in the Mewar Residency and in Danta State. In the volume on Mewar Residency of Rajputana a mention has been made of the Garasias at several places. At all places they have been treated as a different group from the Bhils.[6]

Thus, The Rajput and Bhil ancestors of the present day Garasias of this taluka secluded themselves in the valleys and jungles of Aravalli hills. In this area, at least, their wanderings ended and a long era of peace prevailed. Here, in the primeval forests, the Garasia immigrants made clearances in the forests and established their villages. Thus, in the heart of deep forests, villages grew up and went on steadily multiplying and spreading over the entire Danta taluka.

### Hierarchical Division

On account of the intermingling of differtent streams of population in varying proportion in the different regions of Danta taluka, there have arisen hierarchical divisions among the Garasias. On the top of the hierarchy are the Garasia Rajputs, who consider themselves descendents of the pure Rajputs. Next in hierarchy are the Garasias who also consider themselves descendents of pure Rajputs but as their ancestors have been eating buffalo-meat, they could not claim to be as pure as Garasias Rajputs. The third and the last position in the hierarchy is of the Bhil Garasias who are considered to be more or less like Bhils. However, even the Bhil Garasia do not like to be referred to with the prefix of Bhil. They also like to be referred to as Garasias only. These hierarchical divisions maintained a social distance from each other just like Hindu castes. Neither inter-marrying nor inter-dinning takes place between them. Due to fear of pollution, Garasia Rajput would not accept even water from the hands of a Bhil Garasia.

### Socio-Cultural Traits and Customs

Due to great dependence on forests, the way of life of the Garasias seems to have originated, developed and flourished in the forest setting. From the point of view of social life the whole Garasia country behaves as one cultural area, as there is a homogeneous social code to which all clan groups subscribe. Every Garasia belongs to a patrilineal clan which is believed to have originated from a legendry ancestor. Now-a-days the chief function of the clan is the regulation of marriage and prevention of incest. In former times, the clan represented a geographical unit as is evidenced from the fact that majority of the families in a village once belonged to only one clan. The ecological balance in terms of numerical strength of various species of animals, plants and other products of the forests around the village had been managed collectively by members of the dominant clan living in a particular village.

The name of the clans are as follows: Rathod, Dabhi, Dungaicha, Solanki, Pargi, Gawar, Parmar, Makwana, Khokharia, Bhumaria, Angari, Vansia, Mali, Gorina, Kharadi, Raidara, Palia, Dhranji, Bhagora, Pichhora, Dungri, Nana Parmar, Nana-Dungaicha and Damor. Thus, we came across a total of 24 clans among the Garasias. No information could be obtained about the association of the clans with any totem, particularly with trees and plants in the forests.

### *Kinship*

The Garasias are patrilineal and as such patrilocal. Although an individual belongs to the father's clan lineage and sub-lineage, he is also concerned with the clan and lineage of his mother. The rules of exogamy apply to maternal relations as well as paternal relations. Thus, the life of the Garasias is conditioned by the membership of two clans and lineages, paternal and maternal. But the paternal kin predominates in all spheres of social and economic activities including proper use of forest products and preventing destruction of forest by others. In seeking help or assistance the kins from the paternal side are first approached and only when assistance or help from them is insufficient, materilineal kins are approached. In matter of fulfilling customary obligations, such as collection of minor forest produce or cutting wood to be used in house construction, the rules of kinship system in Garasia society expect the kin from paternal side to act first.

### *Family*

Ideally the basic residential, socio-religious and economic unit is the patrilocal extended family. This consists of man, his wife, his sons and their wives and their children plus unmarried sons and daughters. Of course, this unit is not supposed to occupy one house. Preferably, they occupy separate houses for each nuclear family consisting of a man, wife and unmarried children. All members share in the family occupation and in the products obtained from the forests. All may not eat from the same hearth. In fact, each nuclear family has its own hearth. Thus, the domestic pattern of the family, in general, is of nuclear type. The average size of family is seven, as found among the surveyed families of the four sample villages.

### *Community and neighbourhood*

The local community is defined as the largest unit of contiguous homesteads which recognise the reciprocal obligation to participate in religious and economic activities. Ordinarily, natural features such as grove of trees, or upland region and plain region define some of the boundaries of this group. Community members are members of the same clan, though they may be of different lineages, and as such part of the village relationships. Such community is made of several neighbourhoods. A neighbourhood is a cluster of households whose members belong to the same lineage and who work in the forest and visit one another more frequently than they do with members of the same community. Although the neighbourhood is a territorial unit of the community, its boundaries may not be marked with any natural features. Though neither the community nor the neighbourhood has any formal organisation or institutionalised leadership, the protection of trees and preservation of the plant species around the community and neighbourhood are being looked after by the members of the community and neighbourhood households.

### *Solidarity*

Although the people of a Garasia village co-operate in work, recreation and ritual and although their relations are conditioned by kinship regulation, they value family privacy and autonomy over neighbourhood solidarity. The village community as a segment of a continuously settled area, with no formal political organisation of its own, does not inspire special loyalty in its members. The settlement of dispersed homesteads has no public place or building as a special focus for group sociability in any village.

Despite the sub-division of the community along neighbourhood and lineage lines, there is, in general, no factionalism as is usually found in the non-Adivasi villages of the taluka. This is partly because the community has too few joint activities around which factions might crystalize. This helps, in a way, in preventing undue cutting of trees and exploitation of other plant species.

### *Social Control*

Leadership in the traditional Garasia society was not institutionalised in set of permanent position with fixed powers. The village Panch is the main structural unit of the Garasia political system in the village. A Panch is composed of the elders and wise persons of the village, who are known for their impartial judgment in the interest of the village. This is not a fixed organisation with fixed membership. But whenever there is any social problems connected with, say, cutting of trees by any villager, the affected party informs the elders and persuade them to take up the problem. A meeting of the Panch is called, which all the wise elders including the Police Patel are asked to attend. This Panch organisation takes the responsibilities of maintaining ecological balance and ensuring that, unnecessary cutting of trees by village members is kept under check. Whenever a family needed wood or timber, it will approach the Panch to obtain necessary permission and approval.

### *Religious life*

The Garasias believe that the fate of the individual and his community depend on their relationship with unseen supernatural powers whose natural abodes are in forest. Due to this, the Garasias would not like to destroy the forest environment because most of their deities stay in such environment. The religious beliefs of the Garasias and their ritual practices recognise the existence of two different sources of supernatural forces. The one centres on beliefs in a host of non-human spirits that inhabit certain places in the forest and the other on veneration of ancestors, who in their divine state after death, control many activities of the living. Under the influence of these two forces, the animistic and the ancestral, life must be conducted in such a way that both remain appeased at all times by worship and performance of rituals as well as by avoidance of actions which might offend these supernatural forces. Destruction of forest around them is one such action which will offend the supernatural forces and hence the Garasias would not indulge in such actions. Similarly, the ancestors, while alive, had been living in forest environment and hence, in order to keep the ancestral spirits appeased, Garasia would not indulge in actions which might destroy the forest environment. In these ways, the ecological balance is maintained by them due to the fear of supernatural and ancestral forces.

Walking through the forested region of the villages, one may find, near a strikingly large tree or between two forested hills, some of the oldest shrines of the Garasias. These shrines consist simply of a pointed stone or an earthenware plaque bearing the figures in a relief of a deity and honoured with flimsy roof of flag sticks. Trees around these shrines are never cut.

*Bakhar Bav Singh* traditionally ranks foremost among the supernatural deities. *Bakhar* is the name given to the hill ranges in the Garasia country. Hence *Bakhar Bav Singh* is the mountain god whose mount is horse and who reside in the forested hills. *Bakhar Bav Singh* is supposed to be protector of the Garasia villages and hence most revered. Due to his fear, no Garasia will unnecessary bring harm to the forest.

The Garasia also belive that a host of ghost or malevolent spirits inhabit the village and surrounding forests. These ghosts are usually the wandering spirits of deceased people who are out to attack the living people. Their fear tends to prevent people from going to forest at night. It is believed that the ghosts wander in the air. However, certain trees are tenanted by them. Their favourite trees are '*ambli*' '*bor*' and '*ambo*'. If a particular tree is recognised as the abode of a ghost, a piece of flat stone is kept underneath the tree which represents the image of the same. For appeasing this spirit, no harm is brought to such trees. In fact, '*ambli*', '*bor*' and '*ambo*' trees are seldom cut by the Garasias.

Due to these aspects of their socio-religious life, a good number of taboos, restrictions and avoidances are observed by the Garasias in cutting trees or bringing harm to trees which, in turn, help in maintaining the ecological balance. Thus, the forest economy of the Garasias and their method of exploitation, when seen aginst the background of their beliefs and rituals, are sound insofar as they usually served their immediate needs and safe-guarded the interests of the wider society in the forests.

## Locational Concentration of Groups

The Garasia Rajputs are concentrated in the villages of northern and north-western parts of the taluka. In two sample villages, viz., Pansa, and Sembalpani, the main tribal community is Garasia Rajputs. The Bhil Garasia are concentrated in the villages of eastern part of the taluka. Other two sample villages Mahuda and Sandhosi have mainly Bhil Garasia population.

From the point of view of social and cultural life, however, the whole of Garasias (including Bhil Garasia) seem to be one cultural unit, as there is a homogeneous social code to which both groups subscribe.

## Other Communities in the Taluka

Apart from the tribals, there are some other communities in the taluka which are backward but are not listed as either Scheduled Tribes or Scheduled Castes. Such communities are Thakarda, Maji Rana, Bhil and Rabari. The Rabaris are mainly found in villages in north-western region of the taluka. Their main occupation is cattle rearing. They are found to live both in tribal as well as non-tribal villages.

Among the Caste Hindus, Rajputs appear to be dominant community followed by Brahmins. Banias too are in fairly good number. Among the Muslim population, Momins have thick concentration in this taluka, followed by Bohras. From the point of view of wealth, the Rajputs and non-Momins appear to be in a better condition.

The population of Scheduled Castes in the taluka is not very large. But quite a good number of caste groups are represented in their population. The highest concentration is that of Bhambhi or Chamar. Next to them are the Bhangis or Mehtar. The third in order are Shenvas. Besides these major groups of Scheduled Castes there are others belonging to caste groups such as Mahyavanshi or Dhed, Garoda, Meghwal, Mang, Turi, Tirgar, Chenna Dasar or Holaya Dasar. Most of these Scheduled Castes are concentrated in the plain region of the taluka. In the hilly region, one does not come across large concentration of these groups. This fact clearly indicates that the number of these groups have settled in the villages where Caste Hindus or Momins are found.

## General Implications of Environment

On account of their environmental situation, the Garasia country has always been insulated to a very great extent against political and commercial activities. The region continued its political and economic seclusion from the plains; both from north Gujarat plains and from Rajasthan plains. Due to uncertain political and economic situation during the Mughal and British regimes, it was not uncommon among the Garasias to migrate from one place to another (of course, not beyond the hills and forests) in search of peace and economic stability. Only after the pacification of whole region through the British protectorate, the Garasias got a general security.

Throughout their known history, the tribals of this taluka have inhabited a broad, scenic mountain valley lying in the Aravalli ranges. Virtually all the material needs of the people were limited to the resources made available by the natural environment. For the satisfaction of two basic necessities of life, viz., food and shelter, the forest environment made them available a variety of forest products.

The entire economic system of these people, although does not revolve round the forest, nevertheless, still it is influenced, to a large extent, by the material sources found in the forest ecology. Despite the large scale replacement of the forest based eco-system by an agriculture based eco-system, the adaptive relationship between these tribals and the forest environment have remained stable and persisted over long period of time.

The daily living of the tribals is inter-woven with rituals and prayers. Their world is populated with spirits and guarded over by a small pantheon of deities. Healing was in the hands of medicine makers and *shamans*, the latter specialising either in diagnosis or curing. Herbal remedies are still not limited to the alleviation of physical ills but could be used to ward off evil and promote good fortune in such a variety of undertakings as hunting, basket weaving, house construction, love making and child birth. These aspects of the Garasia culture have survived the 20th century though its importance is diminishing fast.

## REFERENCES

1. Sherring, M.A., "*Hindu Tribes and Castes,*" Calcutta 1881.
2. Grierson, G.A., *Linguistic Survey of India*, IX, III.
3. Forbes, Alexander, K., Rasmala. *Hindu Annals of the Province of Gujarat in Western India*, Oxford, I, (1924). (Bhil languages), Delhi, 1968.
4. Forbes, Alexander, K., Op.cit.
5. Venkatachar C.S.(1931). *Census of India*, I, III, GOI, Delhi.
6. Erskine, Lt.-Col. K.D., "*Rajputana Gazeteer, Mewar Residency,*"

# 4

# ENVIRONMENT AND MATERIAL TECHNOLOGY

THE TRIBAL community of this region derives economic resources, material technology, medicinal needs and social and religious requirements from the forest around them. Their relationship with forests has not changed much. Though they are now exposed more frequently and powerfully to the people having modern material culture, their own culture and material technology has not changed in a remarkable way. This could be seen from the discussion regarding use of materials and technology in selecting a village site, constructing the residential space, use of household goods, farm implements, activities, like, hunting, and musical instruments.

## The Village Site

The Garasias build their houses just near their farms. The houses show a scattered pattern within a village area. Due to such a nature of village settlement it becomes impossible to comprehend the actual spread of a village. It becomes difficult to differentiate between two village boundaries which, at times appear to be emerging due to this pattern of settlement. The village morphology of Garasia community is similar in all villages, especially so in case of layout and scatteredness of houses. Due to unfavourable geographical conditions, perhaps finding many suitable sites for house construction in a contiguous manner is difficult. The newly constructed school building, *panchayat* office or *gramsevak* residential quarter are the only alien landscape features in a typical Garasia village of this taluka.

Most of the land in the villages is under rainfed cultivation, growing cereals and maize. The rest of the surrounding land covers uncultivated and rocky pastures. The villages of northern and central parts of Danta taluka have greater proportion of their land under forest cover including the sample village of Pansa and Sembalpani. However, in the eastern region, the villages do not have forest cover as such but one finds scattered scrub-lands.

The villages of northern part of the taluka are situated in a plateau like region cut by sharp valley and escarpments. The sites of most of the houses of these villages lie on the slope of the escarpments. The network of paths show efficient connectivity of houses. These villages do not have even rudimentary road plan that one finds commonly in most of the Indian villages. As the narrow strips of paths run through the agricultural land, it becomes difficult for a newcomer to find an approaching road to, any particular house during the agricultural season.

Now the majority of the Garasia villages are connected by *pucca* roads which have been constructed by government under the programme of restoration of communication. There will be only a few houses located on either side of a newly built road and not necessarily close to the road. In majority of the cases, houses are far away from the road and remain unsighted due to the local topographical features. In fact, the houses located in the upland of the villages are completely obstructed by high cliffs. The rise of rocky. land stretching discontinuously obstruct the entire view of a Garasia village.

The probable reasons for building scattered houses are:

(i) The fear that their neighbour may invoke evil spirits and bring some calamity on them,

(ii) Their great dread of infection, which they believe to be the work of evil spirits and

(iii) There is always the fear of catching fire if the houses are close to each other, considering the material of which they are made.

**The House and Court-yard**

Each nuclear family typically maintains sleeping and cooking arrangements and eats apart from the others while it shares the courtyard and engages in a number of common activities within the compound. However, it is not necessary for the siblings to live together in a common compound. Each one may erect a separate house with a provision of courtyard. Both these types of dwelling units are common among the tribals of this taluka. The systems of exclusive and shared compounds co-exist.

The arrangement of the compound is almost uniform and always includes a house for each family. In case of only one long house, having two or three rooms in a row, with a common verandah, even the verendah may be partitioned to make two or three separate houses. Generally these houses have only one roof.

The courtyard is bounded on all sides by fences made of green bamboos along with their leaves and twigs mainly drawn from the local environment. The Garasia of Sandhosi village, however, do not now erect such fences around their houses as it has become difficult for them to get bamboo because of almost total disappearance of forest in the region. One wonders, if they could have raised poultry, had this facility of bamboo been available to them, as it could have provided protection to the poultry from other carnivorous fauna.

The fence is constructed in front of the house so closely and in a semi-circular shape that the house inside is almost invisible from outside. The backyard of the house is sometimes not fenced. Fence on the front side has a movable bamboo gate at the centre or near the wall of the house. In the centre of the courtyard, a high level, i.e., seven or eight feet tall wooden platform is made which is well suppeorted by four, six or nine wooden poles. It is known as '*Daglo*' in the local language. It is used for various purposes, such as stacking hay for cattle, for drying grain in the sun, etc. The platform is reached by a wooden ladder. The pillars which support '*Daglo*' are known as '*Thamba*'.

In the corner of the courtyard, attached to the front side wall of the house, a raised wooden structure is usually provided to keep earthern pitchers for storing drinking water. Washing of utensils and bathing is done in close proximity of this stand and hence the problem of drainage does not arise. As the houses are built on elevated ground or slopes of small hills, the rain water and domestic waste water drains away. The floor of the house and courtyard is broomed twice or thrice a day in order to give the house and courtyard a tidy look. Some evergreen plants thrive by taking advantage of the domestic wastes including drainage water in the corner of the courtyard. Walls of all the houses are built with mud and roofs are covered with country tiles made by the local people. The house is generally rectangular having one living room, with one door. Not a single window is provided for ventilation. Hence the interior of the room is quite dark even during a day time. Walls are made of brushwood of opened bamboos, plastered inside and outside with a mix of mud and cowdung. These building materials are drawn from forests, agricultural fields and livestock population.

Construction of a house is a simple affair. A frame of wooden pillars (mostly of 'Khair' and teakwood) is fixed up first and then the bamboo planks are fitted in-between the pillars to make the wall. Over the wall, a structure is built by wooden rafters and bamboos. Over this, the roof is covered with hand made flat tiles '*adobe*'. However, The Garasia of Sandhosi and Mahuda villages do not make such flat tiles by themselves. They use country tiles which are made by craftsmen belonging to the potter caste.

Not everybody is expert in making *adobe*. If members of a household are not able to prepare them, they get them prepared by somebody in the village who knows it. The kinsmen do help each other in making the *adobe* as these cannot be manufactured single handedly. The required clay is collected from a pond, which is in a drying state, it is mixed with water and kneaded thoroughly into a smooth mud-paste. The mud-paste is put into a rectangular frame for giving the flat shape to the tile. After taking out the paste from the frame, it is kept in the open for sun-baking. As there is extreme heat in May, it is considered to be the proper month for manufacturing *adobe*. Sometimes they do bake the tiles with the help of fire. Firewood for this is collected from the jungle.

Roof of a house is set on heavy rafters that are hand cut. These beams form the frame for the tiles. Logs of wood are brought from the forest and are later cut into beams by hand. Tools used for this cutting and shaping are also primitive. The beams and rafters are generally of Khakhra (Palash) tree. The main beam is called '*Pat*' while the middle long beam in the room is known as '*Mador*'.

But, the most important single material for the Garasias in the construction of houses is bamboo. It is also used for a number of other pruposes such as ceiling, walls and fencing of the courtyard.

'*Athir*', the horizontal beams along the top of the room, form a space used for storage. These horizontal beams are supported by four or six wooden poles which are known as *Tirpaya* and the bamboo frame which is put across the horizontal beams is known as *Khatbi*. No two-storey house is found in any Garasia village. The walls are generally plain and simple without any paintings or carvings.

The general pattern of the houses indicates one living room, Ghar with a Verandah, i.e., *paithar*, on the front side. The living room is usually one step higher than the Verandah. Sometimes, the ground level of the outer fringe of the Verandah is raised which may be used for sitting purpose. In some houses, having such raised ground level of

Verandah, the screens made up of long thin strips of bamboo are fixed on the raised ground. The screens touch the roof of the house and thus the Verandah is also converted into another room. If the Verandah has such enclosures, a bamboo plank, serving a purpose of door, is also fixed. This is mainly done to prevent animals from entering the Verandah.

But there are houses even without a Verandah. Most of the houses in the village are one-room houses. A few well-to-do households have two-room houses. But every house, which has two rooms, practically are two houses with a common wall. This means that Garasia do not construct such houses in which rooms may be connected. Whenever, an individual wants to add another room, he does so by extending the back and front walls of the already existing room and erecting a roof over the extended walls, after constructing the side wall. Usually the second room is erected for allotting a separate unit to a married son or a married brother. The floor space of the living room (including the verandah) is usually between 20′ X18′ to 25′ X20′.

The living room is used for all purposes. The cooking place is also inside the living room. A semi-permanent *chula*, a mud oven, is built in one corner of the room, generally towards the wall on the right side. These *chulas* emit smoke which spreads in the room as, so far, the smokeless *chulas* are not introduced here. In some houses *chulas* are not built but three big slabs of stone are placed at regular intervals in a semi-circular or triangular pattern which serves this purpose. Even if a house has got a mud oven, the household keeps the above alternative arrangement in the Verandah, generally for the benefit of guests.

The living room is also used for storing maize and agricultural produce along with the household articles. If the house has a Verandah compound, the domestic animals are tied there. In the absence of Verandah, they share the living room along with the family members, particularly during winter and monsoon nights when the livestock need a cover. During summer they are sheltered beneath *Daglo* in the courtyard. Both the living room and the Verandah are used for sleeping purpose. Guests are usually received in the Verandah.

The Garasia housewives keep the floor of the living room and Verandah tidy by applying the mixture of cowdung and clay at regular intervals. As such, the floor is rarely found dirty and worn out except in rainy seasons. During this season, due to water splashing on it the mud base washes away. It could not be repaired, as the new plaster cannot dry out immediately.

Inside the living room, towards the western and eastern walls, there are two raised mud altars which are dedicated to supernatural spirits. These are the sacred centres inside the house.

Several wooden pegs are fixed, at the height of 4 to 5 feet, inside the walls at different places. They are used for the purpose of keeping things hanging so that the articles remain out of reach of rats, dogs and small childern. Sandhi, Ginelina, Maju, etc., are wood species used as wooden poles, planks and frames in construction of the houses.

## Household Goods and Furniture

### *Furniture*

It is rather difficult to find an object worth the name of furniture in the houses of the Garasia, except one or two sleeping cots, i.e., *Khatlas* or *Mocho*, which every household possesses. The *Khatla* or *Mocho* is made by the family members of each household for its own requirement. But usually not more than two *Mochos* are kept in the house. As such the adults use the cots for sleeping while children sleep on the floor. A husband and wife usually share the same cot. Cots are generally smaller in length so that the legs of an adult person, if the body is fully stretched, hang outside the cot. The Garasias believe that only the dead lie on a full-length cot.

The cot has a frame with four legs, the open space is covered by the inter-weaving of thin strings made of sabai grass. At one end it is left open where the people use strong and thicker ropes to tighten the woven strings. In former days, the open space within the frame was covered by inter-weaving of thin bamboo strips. A few households still possess such sleeping cots.

One or two mattresses, not very thick ones, are also possessed by every household. These are spread over the cot while sleeping. Pillows are not used by them. Usually some piece of cloth is kept beneath the head which serves as pillow.

### *Household Utensils*

Among the household utensils possessed by the households the most important is *Thali* or the dinner plate of brass metal. There are two types of these plates. The bigger one with smaller elevated rim is used by adult males and females for eating purpose. The smaller one with higher elevated rim is used by children. The higher rim saves the cooked meal from falling out on the floor. They have also pots or cups — which they use for serving cooked pulse or vegetable curry. Brass *Lota* or spherical water jugs are used for drinking water and washing mouth and feet. Only one or two sets of all these brass utensils are possessed by an average Garasia household. As the Garasia's staple diet is bread of maize, they managé to eat the bread by holding it on the palm of one hand. Surplus bread is stocked in a small bamboo basket. Only when pulses or vegetable curry or mutton curry is cooked, they use the brass *Thalis* or pots.

For baking the bread, '*tawa*' is used which is an earthen disc. Some use iron *tawa* also. For kneading the dough they use a wooden plate which is known as *Kathrot*. For cooking pulses, vegetables or meat, each household possesses one or two low cost aluminium utensils and one or two *Pavala*, i.e., brass cups for drinking water and other liquids.

The earthen wares are made by the local potters. The common and useful wares are *matla* - a pitcher—and *lota*. Those who cannot afford to buy brass *lota*, use earthen *lota*. A household usually possesses three or four pitchers of various sizes for storing water in the house.

Women bring water from the well either in earthen pitchers or in iron-buckets but not all the households possess iron-buckets. Nearly all the households possess *ghanti*, the grinding stone. The grinding stone is kept raised over a big circular disc type structure, which is known as *thaliyo*. The flour, after being grounded, trickles down in this *thaliyo* from where it is finally collected. A small broom known as *bali* is also used for collecting the flour.

## Basketry

Basketry consists of bamboo baskets of various sizes and shapes. The most common is *supda* or the winnowing-fan to be found in every household. *Topla* or large circular basket is used for carrying grains from the field to the house or for carrying other articles. It is also used for carrying manure to the field. Several small baskets are kept for storing baked breads, other edibles, fruits collected from forests, etc.

## Other Household Possessions

For keeping the house lighted after evening the Garasias use kerosene which is used in tin lamps. These tin lamps are having open uncovered flame. It is sparingly used. The daily routine is generally adjusted to the day light condition. Lantern has not yet come into vogue.

Formerly, raincoats made out of narrow strips of bamboo were used, but now-a-days umbrellas are used by almost all houses in the village.

Fancy goods such as a mirror, a comb, soap, perfumed oil, etc., can also be found in most of the households.

One or more knives - *chhari* — of different sizes are possessed by every household. Rather, every male, whether he is a boy or an adult, always keeps a knife in his possession.

For churning butter milk, some households possess wooden churner which is known as *kho*.

**Farm Implements**

Among all the agricultural implements the plough share — *har* — and the sickle — *datardu* — are the most important for the Garasias. The iron har is fitted in the wooden plough. It is this part of the plough which tills the soil. This needs occasional sharpening. This is taken to Ambaji where the services of blacksmiths are available. The *datardu* is used for cutting paddy and grass. The *har* is made by these tribals by using the wood of trees such as baval, ankol, bor, khair, limdo, vad, sajija, ponch, sag and garmala.

The wooden shaft of the plough measures about 6' to 8' in length. At the other end is fixed a wooden piece. It is fixed by making a hole in the centre and the shafts are at right angles to each other. The wider end is slightly curved inwards. The upper end is an oval shaped wooden piece which serves as handle. The man behind the plough holds this handle and exerts pressure as required at the time of ploughing. The other agricultural implements used are (i) *Karab* - leveller (ii) *Samar* - leveller and (iii) *Kuhadi* - iron axe.

Besides these, those who irrigate their fields possess *Kosh* - water mot. There are a few other smaller implements such as *Rap*, *Mehre*, etc.

For driving out the birds from their maize and bajri fields the Garasias use *gofan*. This is a circular leather belt with a wide leather piece in the centre for holding a stone. A loaded *gofan* is circled on the head and one end of the belt is let off to give a momentum and direction to the stone.

## Hunting Weapons and Fishing Implements

The principal weapons used for hunting are *tir-kamtha*, i.e., arrow and bow, the scythe, the sword and *lakdi*, i.e., sticks of different sizes. The *kamtha* consists of a thin bamboo and a string and the *tir* is made of reed-shaft generally with a pointed iron-arrow. Of late these *kamtha* and *tir* have very little use for them.

*Dhariya* is an axe consisting of bamboo or wooden pole which is about a-yard-and-half long. It has a sharpended iron blade which is fixed into the wooden pole by means of a hole at the other end of the blade. Every Garasia household possesses a sword, i.e., a *Talwar*. It is customary for an adult Garasia to carry a *Talwar* in a sheath, hanging on the side around the waist. *Talwar* is carried as an item of personal decoration, although they point out that they carry it to protect themselves from wild animals or an enemy. Besides it, every adult Garasia carries a Rampuri *Chaku*. This Rampuri *Chaku*, a sharp, long and strong knife, is always found on the body of a Garasia, tucked inside the *dhotli*, i.e., the loin cloth on the waist. Knife is also kept in a sheath. Besides these two weapons, a few Garasia households also possess a rifle. Fishing implements consist of bamboo traps of different kinds and sizes.

## Musical Instruments

The Garasias have a great fancy for music and dance. On several religious and marriage occasions dancing and singing are invariably held. Songs sung in the praise of deities are sometimes accompanied by dancing. Seldom is a song sung without accompaniment of musical instruments. The most important musical instruments for them is *dhol*, i.e., a drum which is eliptical in shape. The two narrow ends of a *dhol* are covered with goat hide.

Another popular and common musical instrument is the bamboo *vahal*, a flute. Most of the young men possess flutes. There are two types of flutes. One is small in size and is known as *vahal*. The other is bigger in size and girth of its body is also larger. This is known as *morli*. *Thali* is also used for keeping beats at the time of dancing. The other important instrument is *nagara* which is a small drum more or less circular shaped. The upper end is covered with strong tanned hide. It is hung on the neck of the player and two small sticks are used for beating. Another small musical instrument is *kudi*. This instrument is made from chips of bamboo. The chips are of different sizes. They are fixed on two wood panels and give different notes when struck by a wooden piece.

Besides these, there are *tali* - cymbals, which are used particularly at the *bhajan* sessions. Another musical instrument, conch - *Shankli*, is used when *bhajans* are sung in the praise of deity like Ramdeo Pir. *Shankli* is a large circular shaped instrument. Only one side of a circular wooden frame is covered with hide. It is played by using the fingers and palms only.

At the *bhajan* sessions held in honour of *Dhule-na-pat* (Bhagwan), the devotional songs are sung on the accompaniment of *temro* - tamburs. *Temro* is a stringed musical instrument.

**Miscellaneous**

The forest in this region has also such plants and trees which provide fibres used by tribals of this taluka for making ropes and cords. For instance, the root-bark of 'khakhra' tree yield a strong fibre called *Chhoel* which is used for making ropes and cords by the Garasias.

Nearly all the agricultural implements which the Garasias have been using, such as tool handles, axes, shafts, pounders, mortars, wheels, carts, ploughs, yokes, etc., are made from wood of a variety of trees. Thus, the forest, which has been for centuries home for the tribal of this taluka, has been a great source in enriching their life.

The Garasias and forest have remained linked with each other since centuries. Looking into the historical background of the Garasias, their eco-system framework clearly indicates the effectiveness of forest environment with respect to their material technology like soil and water, the forests have always been a significant resource for them. Restricting the use of forest is irksome to them. Any restriction and regulation brings insecurity to them and they try hard to shake off the restriction.

# 5

# FOREST

DANTA TALUKA once had thick forests. The shoulders of the hills and valleys between the spurs were thickly covered with good natural forests. Increasing population pressure and the resultant over exploitation of forests have taken a heavy toll of the forests. This process was initiated in the pre-independence India and continues even today. All felling, however, is not always authorised.

The feudal rulers of the area had executed contracts for the harvesting of trees. These were guided by the exigency of immediate revenue requirements. They were detrimental to the principles of forest conservation. Some modifications were made in the contracts after independence, which were as follows:

*Timber and Fire-wood Contracts*

Steep slopes were exluded from felling. Twenty-five per cent of the remaining trees standing in the forest areas were to be preserved. Nineteen tree species were declared reserved. Besides, these species all trees of khakhra or palas, i.e., *Butea monosperma* under 12" girth at breast height (dbh.) were also retained.

*Katha Manufacture*

All khair, *Acacia catechu* of 12" dbh., were also reserved. Though these modifications were introduced, it was found to be difficult to implement them. Unauthorised felling of these trees took place. This led to wide-scale degradation of forests in this area. Eastern part of this taluka (where two sample villages, viz., Mahuda NCS and Sandhosi NCL, are located) suffered more serious losses.

Large chunks of forest area in the north and north-west part of this taluka were reserved from felling by the feudal kings as '*shikar*', i.e., hunting regions. Hence, they have survived the axe of the contractors (two sample villages, viz., Pansa CS and Sembalpani CL belong to this area).

## Forest Type and Species

The forests in the Danta taluka are dry deciduous, scrub type forests. Hardly 10 per cent trees are of teak variety, hence this becomes a dry deciducus non-teak forests area.

The forest cover has natural growth of three layers. The top-layer is of height of 8 m. and more. The middle-layer is composed of scrubs of 2 m. to 8 m. and the bottom layer is composed of growth up to 2 m.

The field observations made under this study show that the following species grow in this region, constituting the three layers of growth.

*Dominant Species in top-layer*

| | *Botanical Name* | *Local Name* |
|---|---|---|
| 1. | Acacia nilotica | Desi-Baval |
| 2. | Acacia senegal | Goladio Baval |
| 3. | Albizzia lebeck | Siris |
| 4. | Azadirachta indica | Limdo (Neem) |
| 5. | Butea monosperma | Kesudo, Khakhro (Palash) |
| 6. | Ficus bengalensis | Vad |
| 7. | Ficus religiosa | Piplo |
| 8. | Mangifera indica | Ambo (mango tree) |
| 9. | Moringa oleiferia | Saragvo |
| 10. | Syzygium cumini | Jambu |
| 11. | Terminalia arjuna | Arjun sadad |
| 12. | Terminalia bellerica | Baheda |
| 13. | Terminalia chebula | Harde |
| 14. | Pongamia glabra | Kanji |

*Dominant Species in top-layer*

| | *Botanical Name* | *Local Name* |
|---|---|---|
| 1. | Acacia catechu | Khair, Katho |
| 2. | Acacia leucocephala | Harma Baval |
| 3. | Adina cordifolia | Haldarvo, Haldu |
| 4. | Albizzia lebeck | Siris |

| | Botanical Name | Local Name |
|---|---|---|
| 5. | Anogeissus latifolia | Dhavdo |
| 6. | Anogeissus pendula | Dhar |
| 7. | Cassia fistula | Garmalo (Amaltas) |
| 8. | Diospyros melanoxylon | Timroo |
| 9. | Emblica officinalis | Amla |
| 10. | Gmelina arborea | Sevan |
| 11. | Lannea coromandelica | Modad |
| 12. | Manilkara hexandra | Rayan |
| 13. | Morinda tinctoria | Aal |
| 14. | Moringa oleiferia | Saragvo |
| 15. | Phoenix sylvestris | Khajur |
| 16. | Pterocarpus marsupium | Biyo |
| 17. | Xeromphis spinosa | Mindhal |

*Dominant Spices in middle-layer*

| | Botanical Name | Local Name |
|---|---|---|
| 1. | Cordia dichotoma | Vad gunda |
| 2. | Cordia myxa | Nana gunda |
| 3. | Limonia acidissima | Kotha |
| 4. | Zizyphus mauritiana | Bor (Ber) |

*Dominant Spices in middle-layer*

| | Botanical Name | Local Name |
|---|---|---|
| 1. | Aegle marmelos | Bili |
| 2. | Alangium salvifolium | Ankol |
| 3. | Boswellia serrata | Gugal |
| 4. | Holarrhena antidysenterica | Indrajava |
| 5. | Miliusa tomentosa | Umbtio |
| 6. | Wrightia tinctoria | Kudi, Runchalo Dudhlo |

| | Botanical Name | Local Name |
|---|---|---|
| 7. | Bambusa arumdinacea | Kantis |
| 8. | Capparis aphylla | Kerdo |
| 9. | Sapindus laurifolius | Aritha |
| 10. | Helicteres isora | Merdasing |
| 11. | Vitex negundo | Nagod |

*Dominant Spices at ground-layer*

| | Botanical Name | Local Name |
|---|---|---|
| 1. | Calotropis gigazntia | Akado |
| 2. | Cassia occidentalis | Kasundaro |
| 3. | Cassia tora | Kuvadio |
| 4. | Zizyphus nummularia | Chanibor |

*Less Dominant Spices at ground-layer*

| | Botanical Name | Local Name |
|---|---|---|
| 1. | Aloe vera | Kuvar patha |
| 2. | Barleria prionitis | Pilokanta shalio |
| 3. | Curculigo | Musli |
| 4. | Dicantheium caricosum | Gundeli |
| 5. | Plumbago zeylanica | Chitrol |
| 6. | Urginea Indica | Wirdonion |
| 7. | Zingiber officinale | Adarkh |
| 8. | Zizyphus mauritiana | Ringa-bor |
| 9. | Zizyphus xylopyra | Ghat-bor |

Besides these, some hardy grasses also come up naturally at this level.

Some species like Borsali, (*Mimusops elengi*), Shimlo (*Bombax ceiba*), and Eucalyptus also appear but they are the results of special plantation efforts and do not come up naturally.

The forests in this area are thus degraded and scanty but they have a rich diversity.

## Forest-based products and their uses by the tribals

Forest provides materials to meet the needs of the tribals with regards to fuelwood, timber, medicine, musical instruments, farm implements, housing etc. Minor forest products also play an important role in their economy. Tribals have also been showing ingenuity in using the rich botanical diversity in curing certain diseases. In using some of the forest based products for agricultural use also they have shown special skills.

The following species are put to the uses as indicated bellow:

*Fuelwood*

Baval, kesudo,. shimlo, ankol, bor, halar, golar and sanoh are the relevant species. Their branches and leaves are used for the purpose. Reliance of the tribals on them is very extensive as other fuel materials are not available in these villages. Besides, the wood is more easily available.

*Timber*

Teak, salti, khair, baval and mahuda species are used as small timber.

*Furniture and farm implements*

Baval, ankol, bor, khair, limdo, vad, sajija, ponch, sag and garmala are the species which are used for the purpose.

*Poles, planks and frames in construction of house*

Wood of khakhro, timroo,limdo, baval, bor, halar, golar, mahuda, sandhi and savan maju are used by the tribals for this purpose. All details regarding the methods of use of process or preparation are not available. These details are provided only where available. Similarly scientific names for all local species are also not avaliable. In such cases they are marked (?).

*Medicinal uses*

The tribals are found to be using the following species for certain common medicinal requirements :

i. 'Patalkola' (?) a wild variety of pumpkin is used for building up a strong body.
ii. Wild onion - (*Urginea indica*) — is used for treating boils.
iii. Kalidudhi (?) is used for accelerating wound healing.
iv. Kurwo (?) is used in the pre-labour stage. Its leaves are boiled in water and applied on the abdomen to reduce labour pains. Roots of this plant are also used to cure constipation.
v. Musli (*Curculigo*) is useful as a general tonic. Its tuberous roots are used as slurry and is analgesic. The slurry is eaten after delivery to strengthen the uterine muscles.
vi. Flower of Khakhro (*Butea monosperma*) are soaked into water to create an extract. This extract is used to bathe a feverish patient to bring the temperature down. This extract has multiple uses. It is also useful in preventing skin disease.
vii. Tanin powder is obtained from the extracts of the bark of Khair (*Acacia catechu*). It is applied inside mouth to cure mouth ulcers. Gum obtained from this tree is used as an analgesic for relieving backache.
viii. Bark of baheda (*T. bellerica*) is used to cure cough and asthama. Its fruit is one of the ingredients of famous 'trifala' which has an important place even in non-tribal Ayurvedic system of medicine. The other two components of trifala are harade (*T.chebula*) and amla(*Emblica officinales*) which also are locally available.
ix. Harade is found to be anti-dysentric. It is also used as a blood purifier.
x. Leaves and flowers of neem (*Azadarachta indica*) are used to cure skin diseases. Juice extracted from its fresh leaves is very bitter in taste. However, it is drunk (usually during the first week of 'Chaitra' month of Hindu calendar - usually April) as a preventive measure against skin diseases. It is also used externally to cure dandruff and other skin diseases.
xi. Bark of pipal (*Ficus religiosa*) is also used to cure skin diseases.
xii. Roots of Ankol (*Alangium salvifoliam*) is used as antidote of poison.

xiii. Leaves of chitrol (?) are iused to reduce body temperature.

xiv. Koshiba (?) is a twiner. Its leaf extract is made into a paste and applied externally to control body temperature. It is also used to cure boils.

xv. Leaves of Adarkh (?) tree boiled in water are applied on boils and other skin diseases.

xvi. Leaves of saragvo - Drumstick (*Moringa oleifera*) are extracted; this extract is found to be effective in curing eye diseases.

xvii. Leaves of Nagod (*Vitex negundo*) are boiled in water and its steam is inhaled to cure common cold and cough. Paste prepared from it is applied on the joints of body to cure gout and rheumatism. Its leaves are kept in pillow cover and it is kept under head to cure headache.

xviii. Wood apples, i.e,. Kotha, (*Limonia acidissima*) are considered good general tonic. It is used to cure fever and also some diseases of the lungs. It is also found to be useful in curing stomach and throat diseases.

xix. The mucilage obtained from leaves of Aliyo *Aloe-Vera* (*Kuvalpatha*) is used as purgative. It is found useful to cure stomach disorders of infants and children. Leaf paste made from it is used to cure sprain of joints. It is also applied externally after setting the fractured bones. The plant is supposed to possess some mosquito repellent qualities. It is hanged on roof tops or ceiling of house for the purpose. It is also used to suppress blisters after burns injury.

xx. Fruits of vicer (?) are used as insecticides. Paste made from its leaves is applied externally on snake-bite as an antidote.

xxi. Bark of Passia (?) is used on skin disease.

xxii. Bark of Arjuna (*Terminalia arjuna*) is used as a tonic for heart.

xxiii. Tambapan (?) is used to heal boils and also for other skin diseases.

xxiv. Ardusi (*Adhatoda vasaca*) is used by taking out its leaf extract to cure cough, common cold and also for the control of temperature.

xxv. Fruit of Marda sing (*Helicteres isora*) is found to have anti-dysentric qualities.

xxvi. Aritha - soap nuts (*Sapindus laurifolius*) is used as detergent. It is also used to wash hair. This is used even by urban girls.

xxvii. White secuta of Vas (Dendrocalamus strictus), known as vas kapoor, is used as a medicine for T. B., etc.

**Miscellaneous uses**

Integration of forests and its products with the tribal life can also be seen from the angle of many other uses to which they put the products collected from forests. The tribals use these products in many walks of their lives.

(i) Musical instrument, like, flute, is made from bamboo. For making drums they use wood from trees like salar, golar, kalor and savan. These wooden drums are covered with hides and skins collected from killing the game which is found in the forested areas.

(ii) During field visit, it was also observed that tribals applied imagination in using wood in various forms for irrigation purposes. Water wheel was made from khair wood. This was in operation for last 22 years. Cordage for the wheel was made from a twiner known locally ask 'chatra' (?). Trunk of tree (species unknown) was vertically halved (bisected) and then hollowed to make a 'U' section to connect water lifted from the well with the field channel.

(iii) A large number of agricultural implements are made from wood available locally. The following wood species were used to make implements shown against their names.

| *Species* | *implements* |
|---|---|
| Alangium | plough |
| Acacia catechu | " |
| Tectona grandis | " |
| Roseo sanjipo | Seed pans |
| Cassia fistula | Agricultural implements |
| Mangifera indica | |
| Acacia nilotica | |
| Ficus bengalnensis | |
| Azadirachta indica | |

(iv) Cottage industries, like, basket and mat, making are flourishing wherever bamboo is in good supply. Tribals also make hunting equipment like *tir* and *kamtha* from this.

(v) Tribals make an extensive use of bamboo in making huts. Generally, bamboo is used both as roofing, as well as wall materials. These are used in conjunction with other supporting wood balis. These balis arc generally of eucalyptus and baval. The roofs and walls are generally thatched with leaves and grasses.

(vi) Bamboo has a much greater role in the tribal life. Besides its uses mentioned above, like flute, cottage industries housing, etc., it has a number of other applications. It is used as a stick, for making toys and also for making containers to store foodgrains. It is useful to make brooms or handles. Tribals thus have made a wide ranging use of bamboo.

(vii) As tooth-brush, i.e., '*datan*', the tribals use tender branches of many tree species. Prominent amongst them are (baval, vad, limdo, kamboi, ankol, kalajo, kesudo).

Thus the tribals have made multiple uses of many tree species which grow locally.

(viii) Flowers of mahuda tree are used to make the country brew.

(ix) Timro (Tendu) for Bidi making

(x) Bark of Khair for making katha to be used in pan

(xi) Leaves of roi, gundeli,(*Dicantheium caricosum*) as fodder

(xii) Leaves of Rajko, Tur, straws of maize, wheat and also cotton capsule as fodder or livestock feed.

**Natural Vegetation in the Villages**

Along with the increase in population there was increasing pressure on land. The decreasing fertility of the cultivable land was also being felt in these villages. The tribals, not practising intensive cultivation, desired more land for extensive cultivation. As a result of which trees and bushes were cut and land prepared for cultivation. This has resulted in the destruction of the natural vegetation of the villages which is seen more particularly in Mahuda and Sandhosi villages. It has now become impossible for anyone to add new land for agricultural purposes by clearing any piece of forest land because '*ek sali*' practice is discontinued. However, till a decade back, there were certain plots under forest department which were brought under cultivation in all these four villages. Such lands, which were released by the forest department in the economic interest of the tribals were known as *ek sali*, as the right for cultivation was granted on yearly basis. Quite a good percentage of cultivable land in these villages was being cultivated on this basis.

All these factors have been responsible for the destruction of natural vegetation in and around the villages except in the up-land of the villages where certain trees, like mango, limdo, tamarind, bor and so on, are found. In Pansa and Sembalpani some date-palm trees are found right in the agricultural field. These trees were planted by the local tribals. There are natural pasture for cattle in most of the villages of hilly region on the slopes of nearby mountains where the forest is comparatively much thicker. However, during summer, cattle have to be stall-fed. During the rains, shrubs and grasses grow in abundance on the upland of the villages and in the forest.

## Fauna

The forest of the Danta taluka was also once rich in fauna. The fauna was varied and included tigers (*vagh-Felis tigris*), chitta (*Falis jubatas*), panthers (*dipdo-Felis leopardus*), stag (*sambar-Ruse aristotales*), bears (*rinchh-Ursurs labistus*), wild-bear (*dukkar-Bus indicus*), antelope (*haran-Antelope bezoartice*), porcupine (*sahudi-Hystri cristata*), hyneas, wolves, jackals and wild cats (*Felis chaus*). On account of the presence of such wild games, the taluka was considered full of good game sanctuaries and was fully exploited by the former princely rulers and chieftains. Now these wild animals have almost disappeared. Presently monkeys swarm near the village sites and in the jungles. Snakes of all kinds and sizes are also found. Variety of birds, common in dry deciduous forests, such as cuckoos, jungle fowls, etc., are also found today. Among the domesticated animals buffaloes, oxen, cows, goats and sheeps are observed. Generally, all tribals raise some of these domesticated animals. Poultry is popular among the tribal population but is taken up on a limited scale only. The threat of wild animals used to be the main reason for not raising poultry on a large scale.

### Climate

The area experiences a sub-tropical climate which is cool and dry in winter and hot and slightly humid during summer. The mean maximum temperature in summer is 35° to 40° Centigrade (May) and the mean minimum is 12° to 18° C (January).

There are three distinct and well marked seasons, summer, monsoon and winter. From December to January, winds blowing from the north-east to south-east carry cold and damp air. March and April offer a pleasant and temperate climate. Mid-summer is often intensely hot.

The rainy season begins in the second week of June and the rainfall is heaviest in July and August. Just before the withdrawal of monsoon, there is a short spell of intense heat. On the basis of the figures for the annual rainfall recorded at Danta, for the last ten years, the average rainfall comes to nearly 83.2 cms. (S.D. =34.55 and C.V. = 42.8%).

### Soils

Soils and their characteristics are of great importance in an agricultural economy. The soil is sandy loam all over in the taluka with varying proportions of loam, having scattered blackish patches which are observed more in the plain area of the taluka. It is very shallow on the hill slopes, almost exposing rocks, and hence difficult for ploughing and cultivation. The deep soil exists in valleys and indentation which is more fertile on account of being less sandy and a bit more loamy. The soil, being very loose in texture, is subjected to heavy erosion as a result of fast disappearing forest, this being particularly in the regions where Mahuda and Sandhosi villages are located. The primitive method of tribal agriculture is also responsible for this.

Erosion is accelerated in the hilly regions, where Pansa and Sembalpani are situated, owing also to the heavy but unchecked grazing by cattle. This practice has resulted into the impoverishment in the nutrient value of the soils as a result of which xerophytic growth is the dominating feature in the hilly tract. The entire tract of Danta taluka is also threatened by the fast encroachment of the Rajasthan desert.

### Cultivable land

The entire cultivated land of the families in all the four villages lie within the village boundary. No individual of these villages owns land outside their own village. The agricultural land is divided into several plots, varying in size from less than quarter of an acre to three acres.

On account of hilly area, the fragmentation of holding is not to the same extent, as it is found in plain areas. This may also be due to the tradition of this society of not distributing land amongst brothers as a matter of inheritance but continuing to cultivate it jointly even while brothers may live separately.

The tribals of this taluka make distinction between the land which is irrigated and that which is not. The former being called *Piyat* while the latter *Bin Piyat*. By and large most of the cultivable land in these villages is unirrigated.

The other type of distinction is between rocky land and plain land. The former is called *pathrah* while the latter is *garha* land. In all the villages, acreage under *garha* land is very limited.

## Irrigation

Due to hilly topograhy of the taluka, irrigation is not easy owing to the low level of water and the rocky soil. Hardly 10 per cent of the total cultivable land in the hilly-tract of the taluka has been brought under irrigation. Construction of wells under the tribal development programme has brought some relief but is no solution to the lack of irrigation facilities in the taluka. Construction of check-dams have also been done at some places but those too have been constructed in a wrong way due to which the dam remains dry for the major part of the year except during the rainy season. One such check dam is in the Pansa village in which, even during rainy season, the water level remains lower than most of the other areas. Thus, well is the only important source of irrigation. The tribals of this taluka have been lifting water from these wells either with the help of persian wheel locally known as *ranhat* or *pavti*. *Pavti* is manned by the cultivators themselves while *ranhat* is worked with the help of the bullocks.

The tribals living in the villages of eastern part of the taluka had been using an indigenous method of irrigating their fields which is a good example of human adaptation to a particular physical environment. In this method they used to check the flow of the mountainous streams by putting a trunk of date-palm trees across the flowing water at appropriate places. Due to this they were able to store the rainy water. During winter season, they used this stored water to irrigate their fields by way of digging channel. As the flow of the stream used to be checked at some height, it was not difficult for them to rush the accumulated water downward towards the field. This was known as the *Saran* method, i.e., the method of gravitational flow. But the whole scheme depends on adequate rainfall. Thus the tribals have proved their great capacity to adjust to the situation while keeping their culture and traditions almost unchanged.

## Rivers

As mentioned earlier, the small but translucent river Arjani rises from Ambaji hills and converges into the Saraswati river and finally runs towards the Rann of Kutch. There are several other rivers flowing from the mountains but they are not perennial and remain dry during most part of the year. These rivulets are indicative of mountain torrents, carrying in their descent a vast volume of alluvial deposit to enrich the soil in the down stream region.

## Drainage

In general, a major part of the Danta taluka is undulating. Even the plains in the southern and south-eastern parts, which are nothing but table lands, are slopy in one direction or the other. Thus, in spite of sufficient rainfall during monsoon, water drains out from most part of the cultivable land except the deeper low lands in the villages. As the soil is sandy, moisture cannot be retained for a long time.

# 6

# ENVIRONMENT AND TRIBAL SUBSISTENCE ECONOMY IN DANTA

THE CLOSE adaptive relationship between the tribals and the environment has enabled them to survive while leading a relatively isolated life in a difficult environment. During thousands of years past it had been possible for the tribal population of this region to rely on forest based activities like hunting and food gathering and doing simple farming. This primitive way of life is fast disappearing now. Thus, for these people greater and most important change took place in their economic activities in the form of subsistence agriculture which was characterised by primitive technology producing just enough quantity of grains sufficient for the household.

Prior to the British period, private and individual ownership of land did not obtain in their territory. One who cleared the forest and tilled a plot of land became the owner of it. They produced and gathered only that much which was needed for the family unit. In case the number of members in the family increased, they cleared another patch of forest. There was no permanent stake in the land and thus, in the traditional form of economic activities, land never was an issue of dispute or warfare. It did not evoke any kind of rivalry between members of the community.

However, during the pre-independence period, the process of exploitation, extraction and land alineation had become deep-rooted in this tribal region. As a result of the historical tragedy of ruthless exploitation of these tribals at the hands of the non-tribals, the process of their pauperisation also started and became a matter of concern in course of time. The relentless exploitatrion of the forests in this region for the benefit of outsiders disturbed the ecological balance and also adversely affected their economic life. The British government, and following it the native State of Danta, refused to recognise the right of original settlement and the right of ownership of land by right of first clearance of forest. This deprived these tribals of one of their rights which had been recognised by the earlier rulers before the Britishers. The tribals of the region were reduced to a position of economic dependency, the process which had started soon after the arrival of Britishers in this country.

Due to these reasons the self-sufficient subsistence economy of these tribals, which was attained after adapting their life in a forest and hill environment, was disturbed. The new system of economy introduced by non-tribals made disastrous impact on their life styles. The result was that slowly the tribals of this region lost control over their economic destiny.

## Occupational Distribution

Although the tribal are engaged in agricultural activity they also depend on forest for their living. This dependence on forests is more pronounced in Mahuda and Sandhosi villages which belong to the northern region. It is true that pioneers of Garasia villages have cleared thick forests for cultivation. Today, for a majority of these tribals, settled rainfed cultivation has become the primary mode of food production. A look into the figures given in the Table 6.1 below clearly points out that land is the major source of employment and agriculture is the predominant occupation.

Comparing the figures of Danta taluka with those of Banaskantha district and Gujarat State it becomes clear that the taluka is almost entirely dependent upon agriculture. It is natural as it is an entirely rural area.

TABLE 6.1: **Percentage distribution of workers in Danta taluka, Banaskantha district and Gujarat State according to Industrial Categories**

| *Sr. No.* | *Industrial Categories* | *Danta Taluka* | *Banaskantha District* | *Gujarat State* |
|---|---|---|---|---|
| 1. | Cultivators | 83.06 | 59.48 | 37.76 |
| 2. | Agricultural labour | 11.00 | 17.15 | 22.82 |
| 3. | Household industries | 0.41 | 2.63 | 2.71 |
| 4. | Other workers | 5.53 | 20.74 | 36.71 |
| | Total | 100.00 | 100.00 | 100.00 |

*Source*: 1981 Census.GOI

## Profile of tribal agriculture

Adoption of new technology and new methods of agricultural practices have taken place, to some extent, among the tribals of the villages situated in eastern region of the taluka. But, by and large, adoption of new agricultural technology and practices appear to be negligible. Some of the known variables which affect a better rate of adoption of the new technology are: rate of literacy, exposure to mass media, occupational aspirations, opinion leadership, etc. They are consipicuous by their absence. By and large, the tribals of this region still stick to their traditional way of cultivation, which has been evolved by taking into consideration the nature of their specific environment. There may be some exceptions, particularly in tribal village like Sandhosi. But it is also true that, for majority of the tribals, the techniques and tools of cultivation are old and insufficient resulting in low level of production. The farm implements in use are made from the basic wood, bamboo and iron, inherited from the neo-lithic days, and are supplemented by animal and human power.

They use lumps of decomposed cowdung or ash of burnt dry leaves (tree leaves collected from the forests) for manuring the fields. Only a few tribals are found to use chemical fertilizers regularly. Some others might have used chemical fertilizers occasionally but generally speaking these fertilizers have gained no popularity among the tribals owing to three important factors:

First, the belief that indiscriminate use of these fertilizers results in destroying the natural fertility of the soil.

Secondly, the tribals believe that the grains produced with the help of chemical fertilizers do not have the same delicious taste as those grown using manure or ash of burnt leaves.

Thirdly, the purchase of chemical fertilizers requires ready and sizable cash whereas decomposed cowdung or tree leaves are locally available and are also free of cost. The tribals also feel that unless there is a good and sufficient source of water for irrigating the field, the use of chemical fertilizer is not rewarding.

There are two annual crops and harvests which govern the work of these tribals and influence the yearly cycle of all activities in the villages. The two harvests include 'maize harvest' in first or second week of October, just after the rainy season, and 'wheat-harvest' in early summer (March-April) before the hot, dry period. These correspond to the kharif and rabi harvests.

*Rainy (kharif) season crops*

Soon after first or second shower, the fields are ploughed thoroughly and are left open for a week or two. Sometimes a week or two before the first ploughing, land is manured with cowdung and other farm compost. Shortly after the long spell of rain begins, the field is ploughed once again before sowing maize and bajri seeds. Maize being the staple food, it is grown over a large area. Land is ploughed by means of wooden plough drawn by a pair of oxen. As the villagers generally have inferior quality of plough and weak oxen, ploughing is not very deep. However, the sowing of maize can be performed with a little preparation of the soil. Seeds are sown by broadcasting or by placing them into the furrows as the field is being ploughed. Towards the end of the long spell of rain, weeds come up which need to be removed. Weeding is done in a maize field with the help of a sickle. By August when all the weeding is finished, there is little to do but wait for the crops to ripen. In October the harvesting begins.

Along with maize, other coarse millets like *bunti* and *Rodra* are also sown. Pulses like *urad* and *thwer* (arhar) are also sown along with maize. The vegetables grown during this season include chilly, hemp and cucumber. *Bajri* is being cultivated since last 15-20 years in this region during kharif season.

*Winter crop and field activities*

While the maize harvesting is in progress, ploughing the harvested field also begins simultaneously for growing winter crops. Stalks of previous crops are cleared. Many a times the plot, in which winter crop is to be raised, is left fallow during the rainy season and hence, in that case, it is not necessary to clear the dry maize stalks and plough the fields harvested of maize. A week or two after ploughing, wheat seeds are sown. Immediately thereafter the field is ploughed again. The *rabi* ploughing and seeding is done between mid-October and mid-November. During December and January, fields are irrigated once or twice. October and November are two of the busiest months for those tribal households who undertake cultivation of winter crops. December, January and February are comparatively easy months. By mid-March preparations are made for the fast approaching wheat harvest. This is a period of intense activity. Rain and hail-storm are not uncommon, so it is important that the harvest is gathered promptly.

The harvest is hauled to the threshing floor, where it is stored in high rectangular piles. The period following the rabi harvest marks another respite from field-work and heralds the beginning of a season for festivities and marriages.

Besides wheat, *jar* (barley) and *chino* are also sown in dry lands by some households. Some others, who have a better irrigation facility, sow gram, wheat and oilseeds in this season.

Practically no cash crop is grown in the tribal villages of the northern region. But in the villages of eastern region, cotton and groundnut are cultivated on a small-scale.

The cropping pattern in the tribal villages of this region shows that maize has remained a traditional crop. This was an easy crop for these forest cultivators to grow as it is relatively insensitive to changes in temperature and moisture conditions. It still occupies the foremost in their agricultural economy.

## Animal husbandry/livestock population and animal products

The bullocks reared by these tribals are unhealthy and small statured. On account of not feeding them properly, the breed of these domesticated animals has not remained strong enough to plough the fields intensively. Further, when one is using the improved variety of new iron plough the weak oxen become unsuitable. Because of the vicinity of the 'forest' area the tribals lead their livestock for open grazing. However, due to continuous over-grazing these areas which are already degraded forests have not remained very productive. It is a common sight to watch young boys and girls taking cattle to the jungle and grazing them on the soil where hardly a blade of grass is observed.

Usually a household having 0.4 to 2 ha (1-5 acres) of cultivable land keeps one pair of bullocks while those having more land are found to keep three or four bullocks. Some households may not have any bullock but they get bullocks of their immediate kin for ploughing on a comrade basis.

Several households tend goats. A few are also found to rear sheep. Goats find a place in religious sacrifices and entertainment of guests. Diviners usually specify a goat of a particular sex and colour for sacrifice aimed at curing disease, for propitiation of gods and godlings. Their orders are always obeyed. A man above average means shows respect to his visiting in-laws or matrilineal kins by cooking goat meat for them. At the end of the harvest, also, households usually celebrate by slaughtering a goat.

Cattle and goats are also important for the purpose of getting manure. Goats' excreta is considered a very valuable source of manure. The Garasias are not fond of milk. It does not form an important item in their daily diet. But households do prepare ghee from the milk of the buffaloes, for selling out in the market. In this manner, some households (a very small number) do earn income from dairying, though *rabaris* in the same area are found to keep large herds of cattle and earn from dairying.

But, as indicated earlier, livestock for the Garasias are a source of exchange entitlement as it has ready buyers and is easily marketable.

### Land ownership and tenure

Size of land owned is an important parameter of the social status of a family. It determines both - availability of food grains as well as size of herd of livestock. However, only 26.7 per cent of the total land is under cultivation, the major part of the land, i.e., 59.2 per cent is classified as forests. Most of the area is degraded forest area. In the tribal tract of the taluka, particularly in the northern region, the percentage of cultivable land to total land is still very low. Apart from major portion of forest cover, quite substantial portion of land shows a rocky exposure and stony waste and cannot be reclaimed for cultivation. Some land used to be released, from time to time, to tribals on *ek sali* (yearly) basis for cultivation. But it has severe limitation as there is not enough land which can be released in this way. On account of this, the forest department has now ceased to release land for cultivation.

Due to the enforcement of Land Ceilings Act, certain amount of land was declared surplus in the tribal tract of this taluka which has been granted to the tribals but major portion of this land is beyond reclamation. From waste land and *Panchayat Gauchar* land, 1856 ha. of land have been given to 1534 tribals at concessional rates.[1] Thus, although some attempts have been made in earlier times to grant more and more land of cultivable nature to tribals, very fact of non-availability of such land on a sufficient scale applies severe limitations on releasing land for re-distribution amongst tribals of this taluka.

The tenure in the *khalsa* or crown land was *ryotwari* and the *ryot* or cultivator generally was undisturbed in his possession so long as he continued to pay his revenue. These tribal *ryots* were proprietors of the soil in the Danta state. They called their land as 'bapota'(meaning inherited from father). This was the most significant, emphatic and cherished phrase in their language.

Under section 73-A of the Bombay Land Revenue Code, which applied here, land transfers between tribals and non-tribals as well as within the tribals is banned without the prior approval of the competent authority. However, due to one reason or the other such transfers did take place. Particularly, in the villages of eastern part of the taluka many tribals have lost their land. Thus, land alineation could not be completely banned as the area had not been declared as a 'Scheduled Area'. Apart from this, on account of indebtedness to money-lenders or traders, the tribals of this region have to mortgage their land in order to get a loan. In a study conducted on the problem of land alineation by Tribal Research and Training Institute, Ahmedabad, it was found, in a Garasia village situated in the eastern part of the taluka, that 39 per cent of total land-holders had to mortgage a part of their land to non-tribal land-owners. Of the total land in this village nearly 15 per cent had been mortgaged to non-tribal land-owners.[2] Occasionally, some elderly persons or dependent persons, who cannot till all their land, rent out some portion of the land to others on a crop-sharing basis. Proportion of such land is very less. But on all such occasions the land is rented to a member of his or her own lineage. The non-tribal farmers have stopped the practice of renting out part of their land to tenants on share cropping basis, as they fear that, ultimately, this will result in loosing it for ever. There is some scope for agricultural development in terms of increase in the crop-yield, provided the constraints, both physical (environmental) and human, are overcome. Thus, it is of utmost necessity to diversify the economic activities of the tribals of this taluka. The importance of agriculture is amply reflected due to the limited scope in non-agricultural occupations. Because of this situation, also, development of forest areas has an important role to play in future.

## Subsidiary occupation

As a majority of the tribal households are either marginal or small cultivators, the pressure on land is heavy and such households are not in a position to feel contented exclusively by depending on land. The average size of land holding is hardly 2 ha. Only a few tribals have land size larger than this. The largest piece of land owned by household is hardly 8 ha. Further, due to several factors such as poor soil fertility, vagaries of monsoon, use of chemical fertilizers and lack of irrigational facilities the tribals get poor yield from agriculture. It is barely sufficient for them to remain healthy and contented throughout the year.

A large number of tribal households have resorted to subsidiary occupations for meeting their minimum requirements. Either the head of the household or any other adult member of the household, or sometimes both, take up subsidiary occupations. Unskilled manual labour, either on farm or in forest, is taken up by a large number of tribals. They also migrate to other rural or urban areas. As urban migrants, they find their place as construction labourers. Working as labourers in marble mines and collecting minor forest products and bamboo products are other activities available to non-migrants. These are their subsidiary activities. It is clear that even in matters of taking up subsidiary occupations, there is not much choice for the tribals but to choose one basically from the primary sector.

For the tribals, there are a few avenues for getting labour work in road construction, in marble mines near Ambaji and in the afforestation programmes. On-going developmental works are also avenues of such employment. But although more and more tribals can find wage-paid employment, they do not exploit the situation to the best of their advantage. Some socio-cultural traits of the tribals are responsible for this. First, theirs is a closely knit society and they believe in mutual help on free and reciprocal basis. A call for assistance is hardly left un-responded. Such help is common at the times of hectic agricultural activities like tilling the soil and harvesting the crop. Secondly, in case of those who pride themselves as Rajputs, a psychological aversion is shown towards all types of menial labour work. They consider it unprestigious. This nostalgic pride has almost become a fossil. However, sometimes, a household may send a female member or an adolescent boy or girl for such work, if it is in a dire need.

The main source of cash income for a majority of the tribals of this taluka is from collection and sale of firewood and other minor forest produce. These are collected from the forest in the neighbourhood of the village. The tribals of the villages of the northern region collect gum, honey, khakhra leaves, temru leaves, dholi and kali musli, kanji seeds, mahuda and other fruits, etc. On a rough estimate it has been revealed that those minor forest produces contribute about 14 per cent of the total income of the household of the tribals. But the tribals living in the villages of eastern region (in which Mahuda and Sandhosi villages are situated) have much little scope for collecting minor forest products as forests have almost disappeared from this region.

Living amidst forests for thousands of years, the tribals of this taluka basically depend on the forest for their economic needs. The tribals who live in or near forests resort to them for most of their needs, like, grazing cattle, collecting firewood and minor forest produce and small timber. They maintain an elaborate and complex relationship with the forests involving their economic, social and religious life. This relationship between the tribal life and the forest reflected in all the important pursuits of their life. However, the greatest value of the forest for the tribals of this taluka is in respect of economic pursuit. The resource base of their economy which had sustained them in the past has now been reduced. Yet, occasional hunting and gathering of edible leaves and the collection of minor forest products bring in cash income. From the khakhra leaves, they prepare *padiya* (leaf cups) and *patrala* (leaf plates) which are in good demand at Ambaji which has a continuous flow of pilgrims. There is also a good market for firewood at Ambaji, Danta, Hadad and other big villages where non-tribals are concentrated. Besides these, bamboo which is used in house-construction in this region, is also a saleable commodity. The tribals, during the summer season, bring loads of bamboo for domestic use. These are also sold away for Rs. 14 or Rs. 15 per piece. Selling bamboo has to be done in a clandestine manner as it is illegal to bring them for other than one's own household use. It is likely that the tribals are used by the outside market forces to harvest bamboo and sell them. The over-harvesting had led tc degradation of its standing stocks.

Besides these, the tribals also collect fruits such as *'bor'* which they sell at Ambaji and Danta. Honey is collected from the forest and sold to the non-tribals at a cheaper rate. Gum, *teruru* leaves, *dholi* and *kali musli* are now sold to the Gujarat State Forest Development Corporation (GSFDC) at the price fixed by the GSFDC for each item. Due to the initiative taken by the GSFDC, the operations of collection have become more systematic.

Season-wise availability of these minor forest produces is as follows:

| | | | |
|---|---|---|---|
| 1. | Temru leaves | - | 15th April to 15th May |
| 2. | Kadaya gum, Salaya gum, Miscellaneous gum | - | November to May, the peak period being March-April |
| 3. | Honey | - | April-June |
| 4. | Aval bark | - | April-May |
| 5. | dholi and kali musli | - | September-October |
| 6. | Khajuri | - | January-May |
| 7. | Khakhra leaves | - | April-May |
| 8. | Kanji seeds | - | March-April |
| 9. | Bamboo | - | April |
| 10. | Mahuda fruits | - | June-July |
| 11. | Mahuda flower | - | March-April |

*Dholi* and *kali musli* are found only in this region of the State and hence lot of importance is attached to the collection of this product. *Kadaya* gum of superior quality is obtained from the forest of this region. The tribals now take much interest in the collection of these products as they have started getting a steady and an assured income from this source.

Formerly, these tribals had been growing lac on khakhra trees. But, this practice has virtually been stopped as it did not fetch good returns or proved to be beneficial from the economic point of view.

The primary survey and enquiry revealed that all members of the family, including grown-up children, go to the forests in search of these products. However, on observation it was found that the involvement of particular members of the family in the collection depended upon the nature of the products. For instance, in the collection of gum, honey, bark, bamboo, etc., which required more time, the male members were involved. While in the collection of leaves, seeds, white and black musli, firewood, mahuda flowers, etc., women, folk were engaged, though this division of work was not rigid. The skills regarding collection of minor forest produce are taught by the older members of the households to the younger ones. The expertise in field botany possessed by the adult is also passed on to the children while they are out gathering various forest products with their parents and other persons of the gathering group. They learn to identify the useful species, their seasons of availability and types of locations and plant associations in which each is found.

## Processes behind the stagnant subsistence economy

From the foregoing discussion, it is clear that majority of the tribal households are engaged in the primary sector of production. In the secondary and tertiary sectors only a small number of households are engaged.

Some of the most important factors and processes for a stagnant subsistence economy of the tribal of this region are as follows:

(i) The habitat of Garasias is comparatively inaccessible due to the nature of terrain and location.

(ii) As there was no pressure of population on land in pre-independence period the Garasias were not forced to seek employment outside their own region and hence were prevented from migrating to other regions in search of employment.

(iii) The Garasias adapted to their environment in order to maximize the chances of survival in an uncertain world by shunning themselves from outside involvement. Even today the present generation of Garasias avoid contact with the agents of the present day government. The Garasias withdrew from meaningful participation with the agents of ruling class because of their ineffectiveness to manipulate the outside world for their benefit. This has resulted in an orientation towards minimization of outside dependence in favour of supplying needs within the family and the local area.

(iv) There has been almost no exploration of mines and minerals in this region which otherwise could have provided an opportunity to them to come in greater contacts with outside world. Whether this could have led to their faster development or not is a moot point as it is found in many similar situations outsiders benefit at the cost of sons of the soil.

(v) Unlike several tribes in the country (such as tribes of north-eastern region of India and Chotanagpur in Bihar State), the Garasias have not come under the influence of any Christian mission. Not much conversion seems to have taken place in this region. Thus, the Garasias have remained away from the force of change usually brought by such acculturative agencies as a part of their technique to lure people.

(vi) Voluntary efforts, by social workers to bring reformative movement (as one finds in the tribal areas of South Gujarat and

Panchmahal districts) also have been conspicuously negligible. Sporadic attempts by social workers have been successfully resisted by the Garasias of the villages lying in the northern part of the taluka.

In stark contrast to the non-tribals of the plain region of this taluka, the backwardness of the tribals is reflected in the structure of housing, clothing, household articles, education, etc. One of the most revealing facts about backwardness of these tribals is the very low rate of literacy. According to 1981 Census, the percentage of literates in tribal population to total tribal population (including 0-4 age group) in this taluka is only 7.82 per cent, 13.78 among males and 1.72 among females. These figures reveal the fact that the tribals have remained much behind the current of literacy flow.

On account of all these, the Garasias have remained inward-oriented. This was expressed in a high degree of economic self-sufficiency of households, fatalistic attitude, a low level of technological innovation and a relatively closed system of economy. The experience of exploitation has forced the Garasias to keep outside participation to the minimum. The nature of their social and cultural life has also been a contributory factor in shunning outside participation. In other words, the community is marked by a relatively low degree of role differentiation and specialisation of tasks.

It appears that the tribals of this taluka have not been able to adjust their economic life to the monetisation of economy in a suitable manner. The slow rate of progress of development programmes and their unsuitability to the tribal way of living has also contributed to their general retardness. Much of the achievements of tribal development programmes are concentrated in villages of eastern part of the taluka, a region which has better concentration of non-tribals and is also more connected to the outside world. A large number of tribal villages, which are lying in the mountainous fastness in the northern part of this taluka, appears to have been left out in channelising their efforts and inputs in the development.

## NOTES

1. Report of I.T.D.P., Palanpur,1979.
2. M.I. Masavi, (1976). 'Problem of Land Alineation Amongst Tribals' (mimeo) Tribal Research and Training Institute, Gujarat Vidyapeeth, Ahmedabad.

# 7

# TRIBALS AND THE ENVIRONMENT

THE MAIN purpose of this sample study is to understand the influence of micro-environmental conditions on the life and activities of tribal people and also to know to what extent the tribal community lives in harmony with the environmental conditions. The important aspects included in present study are land-use, cropping pattern, size of holding, agricultural inputs, source of income, economic interaction, duration and distance of migration, household assets and various population characteristics. These aspects are studied by selecting four sample villages from two different micro-geographical environments. They were hilly, rugged area with relative high average altitude (430 m.) and forest cover. Sample villages Pansa and Sembalpani fall under this category. Another area is one with relatively low average altitude, (240 m.); greater availability of arable land and scanty scrub-land. Sample villages Mahuda and Sandhosi fall under this category.

The Garasia tribal community in these two different micro-geographical environments shows different socio-economic characteristics due to the inherent geographical difference as it could be seen from the following analysis.

## Population Characteristics

Danta taluka has 6.11 per cent of the total population of the Banaskantha district living in its 186 villages. The four sample villages accommodate 2.46 per cent of the total population of the taluka. These sample villages have an average of 93 per cent tribal population which ranges from 75 per cent in Sembalpani to 100 per cent in Mahuda village as shown in Table 7.1. As against this, it is 45 per cent in Danta taluka and 6.14 per cent in Banaskantha district. The salient population characteristics of Danta taluka show an increasing percentage of tribal population (42 to 48 per cent) and expansion of literacy (9 to 20 per cent). It also shows an increase in the proportion of agricultural labourers (1 to 3 per cent) and percentage of non-workers (55 to 70 per cent) during the decades 1961-81. During the same period, percentage of Scheduled Caste population decreased slightly from 4.54 to 4.26 and percentage of total workers also decreased from 45.4 to 29.9. Similarly the percentage of cultivators decreased from 35.67 to 19.72 and that of other workers from 8.63 to 7.13.

TABLE 7.1: **Population Characteristics of Sample Villages - 1981**

| *Sample villages* | *Geographical Area in ha.* | *population 1981* | *per-cent of tribal population* | *Density of population per ha* | *Female Ratio* | *Per-cent-of literacy* | | *Dependency Ratio* | |
|---|---|---|---|---|---|---|---|---|---|
| | | | | | | *M* | *F* | *M* | *F* |
| *Hilly Region* | | | | | | | | | |
| Pansa | 1385.04 | 887 | 91.87 | 0.64 | 920 | 7.8 | 0.7 | 0.9 | 1.97 |
| Sembalpani | 1542.48 | 482 | 75.1 | 0.31 | 854 | 16.5 | 5.4 | 0.6 | 28.50 |
| Sub total | 2927.52 | 1369 | 86.1 | 0.46 | 896 | 10.9 | 2.3 | 0.8 | 3.1 |
| *Plain Region* | | | | | | | | | |
| Mahuda | 536.49 | 260 | 100.0 | 0.48 | 1097 | 26.6 | 11.0 | 0.85 | 136.0 |
| Sandhosi | 563.45 | 1078 | 98.9 | 0.99 | 925 | 26.3 | 2.7 | 1.14 | 30.9 |
| Sub total | 1099.94 | 1338 | 99.2 | 1.22 | 971 | 26.3 | 4.36 | 1.1 | 39.4 |
| Total | 4027.46 | 2707 | 92.7 | 0.67 | 932 | 18.4 | 3.4 | 9.2 | 6.7 |
| Danta | 86042.58 | 101845 | 45.1 | 1.18 | 946 | 31.0 | 9.8 | 0.9 | 13.4 |

*Source* : *District Census Handbook*, Banaskantha, Gujarat, and Village Records

Danta taluka covers an area of 860.4 sq. kms. (4.68 per cent of the district area) and accommodates 101,845 persons (1981). This gives an average density of 118 persons per sq. km. As against this the four sample villages cover an area of 40.27 sq. kms. and accommodate 2,707 persons with an average density of 67 persons per sq. km. The two sample villages from the hilly terrain are larger in geographical area (average size, 1459.26 ha.) as compared to the other two villages from relatively plain area (average size 549.97 ha.). The four sample villages constitute 4.68 per cent of the geographical area and as indicated earlier 2.46 per cent of the total population of the taluka.

The salient population characteristics of the villages situated in the hilly region are low density of population, low female proportion, low literacy including female literacy and low dependency ratio (including female dependents) as compared to the sample villages of plain region and also relative to the taluka figures. The situation is associated with the productivity of the land, accessibility and communication with other settlements (especially urban) and economic opportunities available within the village.

## Land-use characteristics

The patterns of rural land-use are invariably associated with micro-geographical conditions such as topography, climate (humidity conditions) and soil fertility. In the present study of four sample villages drawn from two different micro-geographical conditions distinct land-use patterns are seen.

The analysis of land-use data within each of the sample villages indicates the dominance of land under forest over in Pansa (87.76 per cent) Mahuda (71.7 per cent) and Sandoshi (50.8 per cent) and the greater proportion of land under non-arable category (93.4 per cent) in case of Sembalpani (includes grazing land). The second important land-use category in all the sample villages is arable land but the proportion is greater in the villages situated in relatively plain area. The interpretation of land-use data, given in Table 7.2 below, becomes more meaningful when we compare statistics between the villages especially in the two micro-geographical categories. The greater proportion of the total land under non-arable category and forest cover (of all the four villages) is observed to be in the villages of hilly region (98 per cent and 73 per cent respectively) that too in one of the two villages (Sembalpani 97 per cent non-arable land, Pansa 73 per cent under forest cover). The proportion of land under agricultural use is 46 per cent in these villages. As compared to these villages, the two sample villages of plain region have 54 per cent of land under agricultural activity. The comparable figures for Banaskantha district and Gujarat are 66.45 per cent and 50.88 per cent, respectively. The settlements in the plain region offer better scope for diversiified land-use pattern. Per household non-arable land and forest land is larger in the sample villages of hilly region (5.74 and 4.77 ha., respectively) and arable land and land under other uses is relatively larger in the sample villages of plain region (1.49 and 0.12 ha., respectively). There is 7.22 ha. of forest land per household in Pansa as compared to 0.67 ha. in Banaskantha district and 0.43 ha. in Gujarat. Again, there is 16.75 ha.

of non-arable land per household in Sembalpani, compared to 0.09 ha. in Gujarat State. Mahuda had 4.37 ha. of forest land per household. This land-use pattern affects the tribals' way of living in a significant way as they determine their major economic activities.

## Household Composition

The analysis of household composition of four sample villages include family size, age-composition, proportion of females in the family and crude dependency ratio (children and aged, i.e., below the age of 14 and above the age of 60). In all, 73 households were surveyed in four sample villages constituting 554 persons including infants and children. Nearly 40 per cent of sample population belong to the family size of 5-8 members; of which 24 per cent belong to the sample villages of hilly region and 16 per cent to villages of plain region. Another 38 per cent of the population belong to the families having the size between 9 and 12. In this category more proportion (22 per cent) belongs to the plain region and relatively less proportion (16 per cent) to the hilly region.

TABLE 7.2: **Pattern of Land-use in Sample Villages**

*(in ha.)*

| *Sample Villages* | *Number of households* | *Arable land* | *Non-arable land* | *Forest cover* | *Other uses* | *Total geographical area* |
|---|---|---|---|---|---|---|
| *Hilly Region* | | | | | | |
| Pansa | 167 | 149.84<br>(10.9) | 12.26<br>(0.9) | 1206.52<br>(87.8) | 4.95<br>(0.5) | 1375.57<br>(100) |
| Sembalpani | 86 | 96.20<br>(6.2) | 1440.26<br>(93.4) | - | 6.02<br>(0.4) | 1542.48<br>(100) |
| Sub total | 253 | 246.04<br>(8.4) | 1452.52<br>(49.8) | 1206.52<br>(41.4) | 10.97<br>(0.4) | 2918.05<br>(100) |
| *Plain Region* | | | | | | |
| Mahuda | 39 | 65.32<br>(27.5) | 1.92<br>(0.8) | 170.46<br>(71.7) | | 237.70<br>(100) |
| Sandhosi | 158 | 228.27<br>(40.5) | 25.63<br>(4.5) | 285.96<br>(50.8) | 23.60<br>(4.2) | 563.45<br>(100) |
| Sub total | 197 | 293.59<br>(36.7) | 27.55<br>(3.4) | 456.42<br>(57.0) | 23.60<br>(2.9) | 801.15<br>(100) |
| Total | 450 | 539.63<br>(100) | 1480.07<br>(100) | 1662.94<br>(100) | 34.57<br>(100) | 4018.46 |

*Source*: Village Panchayat Office, Danta.

TABLE 7.3: **Per household land in different land use categories**

*(in ha.)*

| *Sample Villages* | *Arable land* | *Un-arable land* | *Forest cover* | *Other uses* |
|---|---|---|---|---|
| *Hilly Region* | | | | |
| Pansa | 0.89 | 0.07 | 7.22 | 0.03 |
| Sembalpani | 1.12 | 16.75 | - | 0.07 |
| Sub total | 0.97 | 5.74 | 4.77 | 0.04 |
| *Plain Region* | | | | |
| Mahuda | 1.67 | 0.05 | 4.37 | - |
| Sandhosi | 1.44 | 0.16 | 1.81 | 0.15 |
| Sub total | 1.49 | 0.14 | 2.32 | 0.12 |
| Total | 1.20 | 3.29 | 3.70 | 0.08 |

*Source*: Field Survey, 1985-86.

Table 7.4 shows that there is a tendency towards larger family size in case of the sample villages of plain region and for smaller family size in case of sample villages of hilly region. This phenomena is more clearly shown in Table 7.5. The average family size in Mahuda (plain region) is 11.4 despite its high literacy rates for both male and female. This is perhaps due to the extent of land availability, differences in land-use and the productivity of land. As regards the proportion of female population, the sample survey reveals results which are in contrast to the Census data.[1] The sample households show higher female proportion (1,051) in the villages of hilly region than the sample villages of plain region (950) which may be due to the short distance and duration of out-migration of males to the nearby settlements in the plain region.

The dependency ratio will be relatively more accurate if it is based on the proportion of workers to that of non-workers rather than on the basis of proportions of age group categories as mentioned below.

$$\text{Dependency Ratio} = \frac{\text{Children + Aged}}{\text{Young \& Old matured}}$$

Or

$$\text{Dependency Ratio} = \frac{\text{Population below the age of 15 and above the age of 59}}{\text{Population in the age group of 15-59}}$$

TABLE 7.4: **Number of persons in sample households by size classes and geographical categories**

| *Size of family* | *Hilly region* | | | *Plain region* | | | *Total* | | |
|---|---|---|---|---|---|---|---|---|---|
| | *Pansa & Sembalpani* | | | *Mahuda & Sandhosi* | | | | | |
| | *P* | *M* | *F* | *P* | *M* | *F* | *P* | *M* | *F* |
| Less than 4 | 25 (4.5) | 11 | 14 | 15 (2.7) | 8 | 7 | 40 (7.2) | 19 | 21 |
| 5 - 8 | 135 (24.4) | 69 | 66 | 88 (15.9) | 44 | 44 | 223 (40.3) | 113 | 110 |
| 9 - 12 | 90 (16.2) | 43 | 47 | 121 (21.8) | 65 | 56 | 211 (38.1) | 108 | 103 |
| 13 - 16 | 14 (2.5) | 5 | 9 | 31 (5.6) | 13 | 18 | 45 (8.1) | 18 | 27 |
| More than 17 | 17 (3.1) | 9 | 8 | 18 (3.2) | 10 | 8 | 35 (6.3) | 19 | 16 |

(Figures in brakets indicate percentage to the total population of the sample households).
*Source: Field Survey*, 1985-86.

TABLE 7.5: **Family size and female proportion in sample households**

| *Name of sample* | *Number of house-holds* | *Total number of fami-lies* | *Average size of family* | *Total male members* | *Total female members* | *Sex ratio villages* |
|---|---|---|---|---|---|---|
| *Hilly Region* | | | | | | |
| Pansa | 20 | 130 | 6.5 | 64 | 66 | 1031 |
| Sembalpani | 20 | 151 | 7.6 | 73 | 78 | 1068 |
| Sub total | 40 | 281 | 7.0 | 137 | 144 | 1051 |
| *Plain region* | | | | | | |
| Mahuda | 5 | 57 | 11.4 | 28 | 29 | 1036 |
| Sandhosi | 28 | 216 | 7.7 | 112 | 104 | 929 |
| Sub total | 33 | 273 | 8.3 | 140 | 133 | 950 |
| Total | 73 | 554 | 7.6 | 277 | 277 | 1000 |

*Source*: Field survey, 1985-86.

Under Indian conditions children belonging to the workers' sections who are below the age of 15 and aged above 59 feel compelled to participate in economic activities. Therefore, the method of computing the proportion of dependents based on later will not be realistic. The difference in the figures by these two methods is given in Table 7.6. Except in Mahuda all three villages show lower dependency ratio by considering the ratio of workers to non-workers than by the method of age indices. This is mainly because of the active particapation of children below the age of 14 and aged persons above the age of 60 in economic activities. The proportion of population in the age groups 0-14 and 15-59 is greater in the sample villages of hilly region than that of the villages of plain region where only the proportion of age group +60 is relatively higher. The dependency ratio is more (0.52) in the villages of plain region than that of the villages of hilly region (0.46). This is again because of the environmental influence wherein the people from the hilly region have to struggle hard for their existence. The proportion of male dependents (0.72) is more than the female dependents (0.34) in plain region as compared to the villages of hilly region (male dependents 0.41 and female dependents 0.52).

**Activity, economic interaction and sources of income**

The female participation in subsidiary occupations (agricultural, labour, households and others) is relatively higher in these sample villages and more so in case of the sample villages of plain region (Table 7.7). Of the total workers 70.8 per cent are female in the village of plain region, whereas the comparable figures for the villages of hilly region is 57 per cent. The household activities are carried out completely by females. Agriculture is another subsidiary occupation where one finds greater participation of women (82 per cent) in all the sample villages. The only occupation where male workers outnumber female workers is menial labour activity (54 per cent) where the nature of job demands muscular strength. However, the female participation in labour activity is not far behind (46 per cent).

TABLE 7.6: **Dependency ratio in sample households**

| *Sample villages* | *Total population sample households (SHH)* | *Total workers in sample households* | *Total non-workers in sample households* | *Dependency ratio of SHH based on workers to non-workers* | *No. of persons with less than 14 age in SHH* | *No. of persons with more than 60 age in SHH* | *Dependency ratio of SHH based on age indices* |
|---|---|---|---|---|---|---|---|
| *Hilly region* | | | | | | | |
| Pansa | 130 (64+66) | 90 (44+46) | 40 (20+20) | 0.44 | 40 (23+17) | 7 | 0.57 |
| Sembalpani | 151 (73+78) | 102 (53+49) | 49 (20+29) | 0.48 | 74 (35+39) | 3 | 1.04 |
| Sub total | 281 (137+144) | 192 (97+95) | 89 (40+49) | 0.46 | 114 (58+56) | 10 (6+4) | 0.79 |
| *Plain Region* | | | | | | | |
| Mahuda | 57 (28+29) | 35 (14+21) | 22 (14+8) | 0.63 | 19 (10+9) | 6 (3+3) | 0.44 |
| Sandhosi | 216 (112+104) | 145 (67+78) | 71 (45+26) | 0.49 | 84 (45+39) | 14 (8+6) | 0.83 |
| Sub total | 273 (140+133) | 180 (81+99) | 93 (59+34) | 0.52 | 103 (55+48) | 20 (11+9) | 0.82 |
| Total | 554 (277+277) | 372 (178+194) | 182 (99+83) | 0.49 | 217 (113+104) | 30 (17+13) | 0.80 |

*Source*: Field Survey, 1985-86.

The spatial interaction of the members of the sample households is of two types namely, place of work interaction and market interaction. In rural areas, for majority of the inhabitants the place of work happens to be the farms situated around the village at a cart drive distance. However, for others who are engaged in non-agriculture activities, such as, handloom, are handicraft activities, households, etc., the residential house serves the purpose of carrying livelihood activities. The tribals who collect variety of forest product move in different interior parts of the roadside forest cover. The market interaction refers to the movement of residents to different nearby villages for the purchase of required goods and also for selling the commodities collected or produced by them. By and large the workers in these sample households work in their respective villages (97.8 per cent). The remaining 2.2 per cent (Table 7.8) of workers migrate to different urban areas. The migrants (2.1 per cent) from the sample villages of hilly region move to nearby places (average 20 kms, range 8 to 30 kms) as compared to the migrants (2.2 per cent) from the sample villages of plain region (average of 75 kms, range 35-250 kms). This is mainly because of the easy accessibility in the plain region and also better access to information system. The migration for work takes place in one of the two villages in each of the geographical categories (Sembalpani of hilly region and Sandhosi of plain region). The duration of migration is relatively shorter (average 6 months) in case of the sample village (Sembalpani) of hilly region than the sample village (Sandhosi) of plain region where the duration of migration is relatively longer (average 10 months). The economic interaction particulary for purchase of various goods of domestic consumption and for selling of agricultural and other produce shows an interesting pattern. The economic interaction of the sample households of hilly region is mainly with Ambaji (Table 7.9) which is known for commericial activities arising out of pilgrims. The physical proximity and assured market for their forest products is also another important factor in the generation of economic interaction. Sandhosi which is one of the sample villages of plain region has greater economic interaction, both for purchase and sale of goods, with Thalvada and to a limited extent with Bodia Talav, Danta, Khedbrama and Sandhosi itself. The interaction of households of Mahuda is only with Hadad. The sample households of the plain region interact with more settlements which shows multiple interaction. The households of hilly region on the contrary show a limited interaction. This is also true in case of the interaction for collection and sale of forest produce (Table 7.10).

TABLE 7.7: **Male and Female Participation in economic activity**

*(in percentage)*

| Sample Villages | Subsidiary Occupations | | | | | | | | |
|---|---|---|---|---|---|---|---|---|---|
| | *Agriculture* | | *Labour* | | *Other* | | *Households* | | *Total* |
| | *M* | *F* | *M* | *F* | *M* | *F* | *M* | *F* | |
| *Hilly Region* | | | | | | | | | |
| Pansa | 9.5 | 19.0 | 23.8 | 4.8 | 4.8 | 14.3 | - | 23.8 | 100 (21) |
| Sembalpani | 2.4 | 16.7 | 16.7 | 16.7 | 26.2 | 21.4 | - | - | 100 (42) |
| Sub total | 4.8 | 17.5 | 19.0 | 12.7 | 19.0 | 19.0 | - | 7.9 | 100 (63) |
| *Plain Region* | | | | | | | | | |
| Mahuda | 4.8 | 9.5 | 23.8 | 14.3 | - | 42.9 | - | 4.8 | 100 (21) |
| Sandhosi | 3.4 | 24.1 | 25.9 | 27.6 | - | 12.1 | - | 6.9 | 100 (58) |
| Sub total | 3.8 | 20.3 | 25.3 | 24.1 | - | 20.3 | - | 6.3 | 100 (79) |
| Total | 4.2 | 19.0 | 22.5 | 19.0 | 8.5 | 19.7 | - | 7.0 | 100 (142) |

*Source*: Field Survey, 1985-86.
Figures in bracket indicate absolute number.

The sample households of Pansa and Sembalpani of hilly region collect various forest products such as fuelwood, gugal, grass, honey, dholi musali, kali musali and bor. Among these, except gugal and to some extent grass (mainly consumed locally) all other forest products find the assured market at Ambaji. The sample households of the villages of plain region also collect a few forest products such as honey, dholi and kali musali, bor and to a limited extent grass, despite its dominant activities based on agriculture and animal husbandry. Some forest products of these villages find market in the nearby settlements, such as, Hadad, Talvadi and Ambaji. Major economic activities of the households differ by their micro-geographical environments. Major source of household income in the sample villages of hilly region is through the sale of forest products (33.5 per cent) especially in Sembalpani (37.5 per cent of its total sources of income), and to a lesser extent in Pansa (24 per cent of its total sources of income). Dairy products (milk, butter, ghee and other milk products) are important sources of income for the households of Sembalpani (40 per cent of the total income). This is due to the higher proportion of non-tribal population (mainly rabari community) and higher per household livestock population (refer Table 7.11.). The agricultural activity is fairly significant in Pansa, which is one of the two villages of hilly region. Forest products and animal products of these two villages of hilly region account for 66 per cent of the total income. In each of these villages separately the income derived from forest product ranks second.

TABLE 7.8: **Place of work interaction**

| *Sample villages* | *Total workers* | *Place of work* | | | *Total* |
|---|---|---|---|---|---|
| | | *In the same village* | *Other villages* | | |
| *Hilly Region* | | | | | |
| Pansa | 90 | 90 | - | - | - |
| Sembalpani | 102 | 98 | 2(30.0 km) (period of 4 months) | 2(8.00 km) (period of 8 months) | 4 |
| Sub Total | 192 | 188(97.9%) | | 4(2.1%) | 4 |
| *Plain Region* | | | | | |
| Mahuda | 145 | 141 | 2 (250 km) Radhanpur ( for 11 months) | 1 (60 km) 1 (35 km) Palanpur (10 months) (for 10 months) | 4 |
| Sandhosi | 35 | 35 | - | - | - |
| Sub total | 180 | 176(97.8%) | | 4 (2.2%) | 4 |
| Total | 372 | 364(97.8%) | | 8 (2.2%) | 8 |

*Source*: Field Survey, 1985-86.
Figures in brakets show distance and duration of migration.

In the sample villages of plain region the important sources of income is agriculture (49 per cent) followed by income generated through the sale of animal products (26 per cent). These two economic activities are inter-dependent and conform with the favourable geographical condition like low altitude, ravine, flat surface, sandy loamy soil and greater availability of underground water. Between these two villages, Sandhosi village earns more (50 per cent) income through agricultural activities than Mahuda village (42 per cent) ; whereas, income through dairy products is relatively more in Mahuda (30 per cent) than in Sandhosi (25 per cent). The sample households in the villages of plain region also get income through cottage industries like spinning yarn for khadi, rope making especially in Sandhosi village.

The average annual income per household is higher in the sample households of plain region (Rs. 6,065 per annum) than those of the sample households of hilly region (Rs. 4,950 per annum); as shown in Table 7.11. In Sembalpani, the average per household annual income is relatively high due to animal and forest wealth and in Sandhosi due to higher agricultural productivity.

**Agricultural inputs and Productivity**

With the increase in size of holding, the per ha. seed cost decreases, except in case of Sandhosi, where seed cost increases from Rs. 147.87 (for land size group 2.01 - 4.00 ha.) to Rs. 159.50 (for the size group of 4.01 ha. and above). Similarly, the average cost of fertilizer decreases with the increase in size of holding only in case of sample villages of plain region; whereas, in case of the sample villages of hilly region, the per ha. average cost of fertilizer varies considerably with the size of holding. In all sample villages the average cost of fertilizer has a greater share (30-40 per cent) in the average total cost incurred in providing agricultural inputs (Table 7.12). In plain region, there is a greater usage of improved seeds than in the hilly region due to environmental,[2] Institutional and technological reasons:[3] The total per ha. cost of agricultural inputs (including the individual cost of seed, fertiliser and irrigation) in the sample villages of hilly region is higher (Rs. 795) than in the sample villages of plain region (Rs.741). Farmers in the hilly region are required to spend 7.3 per cent more on farming as compared to those in the plain region.

TABLE 7.9: **Economic Interaction -Purchase and Sale of Goods**

| *Geographical region/Sample villages* | *Total No. of sample house holds* | *Ambaji* | *Sembalpani* | *Sandhosi* | *Hadad* | *Talavadi* | *Bodia talav* | *Khedbr-ahma* | *Himmat nagar* | *Danta* |
|---|---|---|---|---|---|---|---|---|---|---|
| *Hilly Region* | | | For Purchases | | | | | | | |
| Pansa | 20 | 20 | - | - | - | - | - | - | - | - |
| Sembalpani | 20 | 20 | 4 | - | - | - | - | - | - | - |
| *Plain Region* | | | | | | | | | | |
| Mahuda | 5 | - | - | - | 5 | - | - | - | - | - |
| Sandhosi | 28 | - | - | 2 | - | 26 | - | 1 | 1 | 1 |
| *Hilly Region* | | | For Sales | | | | | | | |
| Pansa | 20 | 20 | - | - | - | - | - | - | - | - |
| Sembalpani | 20 | 20 | 4 | - | - | - | - | - | - | - |
| *Plain Region* | | | | | | | | | | |
| Mahuda | 5 | - | - | - | 5 | - | - | - | - | - |
| Sandhosi | 28 | - | - | - | - | 23 | 2 | 1 | - | - |

*Source*: Field Survey, 1985-86.

(*Note* : Figures shown under different places do not equal the total number of households as there are multiple answers).

TABLE 7.10: **Sale of Forest Products**

| *Sample villages* | *Place where it is sold* | | | | | |
|---|---|---|---|---|---|---|
| | *Fuelwood* | *Gugal* | *Grass* | *Honey* | *Dholi/kali musli* | *Bor* |
| *Hilly Region* | | | | | | |
| Pansa | Ambaji | Pansa | Pansa Ambaji | Ambaji | Ambaji | Ambaji |
| Sembalpani | Ambaji | Sembal-pani | Sembal-pani | Ambaji | Ambaji | Ambaji |
| *Plain Region* | | | | | | |
| Mahuda | - | - | - | Hadad | Hadad Ambaji | Hadad |
| Sandhosi | - | - | Sandhosi Thalvada | Thalvada | Hadad | Hadad |

*Source*: Field Survey, 1985-86.

TABLE 7.11: **Per Household Annual Income through different source**

(*in Rs.*)

| *Sample Villages* | *Sources of Income* | | | | | | |
|---|---|---|---|---|---|---|---|
| | *Agricul-ture* | *Labour* | *Forest products* | *Animal products* | *Cottage indust-ries* | *Migra-tion income* | *Total* |
| *Hilly Region* | | | | | | | |
| Pansa | 1219(41) | 590(20) | 704(24) | 431(15) | - | - | 294 |
| Sembalpani | 1098(16) | 439(6) | 2609(38) | 2788(40) | 2(0.03) | - | 699 |
| Sub total | 1158(23) | 514(10) | 1656(33) | 1610(33) | 1(0.02) | - | 494 |
| *Plain Region* | | | | | | | |
| Mahuda | 1644(42) | 628(16) | 400(10) | 1150(30) | 64(2) | - | 380 |
| Sendhosi | 3222(50) | 1166(18) | 50(0.8) | 1645(25) | 296(5) | 75(1) | 649 |
| Sub total | 2983(49) | 1084(18) | 103(2) | 1570(26) | 261(4) | 64(1) | 600 |
| Total | 1983(36) | 772(14) | 954(17) | 1592(29) | 124(2) | 29(0.5) | 5466 |

*Source*: Field Survey, 1985-86.

The average yield per hectare and the size of holding in the sample villages show a negative relationship.

TABLE 7.12: **Average Yield by Size of Holding**

| *Village* | *Average yield (kg.)* | *Average size of holding (ha.)* |
|---|---|---|
| Pansa | 620.8 | 1.31 |
| Sembalpani | 1564.9 | 0.59 |
| Mahuda | 223.9 | 2.72 |
| Sandhosi | 733.8 | 1.64 |

The average yield per hectare is high in the sample villages of hilly region (916.8 kg per ha.) than in the sample villages of plain region (617.3 kg. per ha.) as shown in table 7.13. This unusual phenomenon is mainly due to high yield rate of agriculture output in Sembalpani village. The crop yield is high in the sample villages of hilly region only in case of wheat and maize crops. Average yield of remaining crops (rice, gram, tur, udad and cotton) is higher in the sample villages of plain region. Oilseeds, such as, tal and castor, and other crops, such as, rayado, kalathi, coarse grains and barley, are grown in smaller quantity in the sample villages of hilly region, whereas garlic is grown in a very small quantity in Sandhosi village. As mentioned earlier, the per ha. cost of agricultural inputs is high in hilly region, which also gives high per ha. agricultural input. It is indeed difficult to explain this pattern of behaviour with the help of information collected under this pilot study. However, during personal field visits it was observed that some non-tribals had started owning some land in a 'benami' fashion, as, under the land alienation Act, the non-tribals cannot own a piece of land in a tribal area. Such 'benami' land owners can be presumed to show a different pattern of behaviour. Only an indepth study can bring out the nature of such concealed ownership or tenancy as the case may be.

## Livestock population and animal products

The average number of total livestock population (cows, buffaloes, goat, bullock, sheep, calves and young buffaloes) is higher in the two sample villages (more so in Sembalpani) of hilly region than the average number of livestock population per household in the villages of the plain region as shown in Table 7.15. These two villages of hilly region provide leaf fodder from trees of forest area and grass required

TABLE 7.13: **Average Cost of Agricultural Inputs**

*(per ha. in Rs.)*

| *Sample villages* | *Agricultural land of sample households (in ha.)* | *Average size of holding (in ha.)* | *Seed cost* | *Fertiliser cost* | *Irrigation cost* | *Total cost* |
|---|---|---|---|---|---|---|
| *Hilly Region* | | | | | | |
| Pansa | 26.2149 (20) | 1.31 | 197.57 | 347.78 | 334.80 | 880.14 |
| Sembalpani | 11.9686 (20) | 0.59 | 114.63 | 317.73 | 175.59 | 609.94 |
| Sub Total | 38.1835 (40) | 0.95 | 171.57 | 338.35 | 284.89 | 794.82 |
| *Plain Region* | | | | | | |
| Mahuda | 13.5773 (5) | 2.72 | 92.34 | 220.56 | 169.49 | 482.39 |
| Sandhosi | 45.8717 (28) | 1.64 | 223.89 | 351.65 | 241.62 | 817.16 |
| Sub total | 59.4490 (33) | 1.80 | 193.85 | 321.71 | 225.15 | 740.70 |
| Total | 97.6325 (73) | 1.34 | 183.13 | 328.22 | 248.51 | 761.87 |

*Source*: Field Survey, 1985-86.

for the sustenance of the livestock (please refer Table 7.2 on pattern of land-use). Sembalpani has an element of non-tribal population (Rabari community) which is engaged in cattle and sheep rearing activity.

The Rabari community owns nearly 70 sheep and 12 goats per household. It also owns a much larger herd of cows and buffaloes. If one considers tribals alone living in three villages, viz., Pansa, Mahuda and Sandhosi, the per household ownership comes to nearly 16 animals. Indeed, this is on the high side. Yet, it is to be contrasted against Sembalpani where, Rabaris the non-tribal, are living. As the livestock is subsisting on forests, one can safely argue that the non-tribals are using forests to their greater advantage. The average quantity of milk produced and sold per household is larger in the sample villages of hilly region (90 litres and 57 litres ). The average quantity of milk produced and sold in a month is lower in Pansa and

TABLE 7.14: **Per hectare agricultural production**

*(in Kg.)*

| *Sample Villages* | *Maize* | *Wheat* | *Rice* | *Gram* | *Tur* | *Udad* | *Cotton* | *Tal* | *Castor* | *Rayado* | *Kalathi* | *Coarse grain* | *Barley* | *Garlic* | *Total* |
|---|---|---|---|---|---|---|---|---|---|---|---|---|---|---|---|
| *Hilly Region* | | | | | | | | | | | | | | | |
| Pansa | 128 | 375 | 5 | 26 | 25 | 14 | 6 | - | 0.7 | 37 | - | - | - | - | 621 |
| Sembal-Pani | 378 | 1111 | 6 | 2 | - | 33 | - | 4 | - | - | 23 | 4 | 5 | - | 1565 |
| Sub total | 207 | 606 | 6 | 19 | 18 | 20 | 4 | 1 | 0.5 | 25 | 7 | 1 | 2 | - | 917 |
| *Plain Region* | | | | | | | | | | | | | | | |
| Mahuda | 71 | 74 | 3 | - | 25 | 7 | 44 | - | - | - | - | - | - | - | 224 |
| Sandhosi | 213 | 206 | 21 | 55 | 36 | 39 | 164 | - | - | - | - | - | - | 0.2 | 734 |
| Sub total | 180 | 176 | 17 | 43 | 33 | 31 | 137 | - | - | - | - | - | - | 0.1 | 617 |
| Total | 191 | 344 | 12 | 33 | 27 | 27 | 85 | 0.4 | 0.2 | 10 | 0.3 | 0.4 | 0.6 | 0.1 | 734 |

*Source*: Field Survey, 1985-86.

Mahuda. Among all the sample villages Sembalpani produces more average farm yard manure (FYM) (518.7 kg.) per household per month but is the only sample village which sells FYM (nearly 93 per cent of its produce). The quantity of ghee produced per household is very less in these sample villages (2 kg. monthly average per household).

TABLE 7.15: **Livestock population per household**

| *Sample villages* | *Cows* | *Buffa-loes* | *Goat* | *Bul-locks* | *Sheep* | *Calves* | *Young buffaloes* | *Total* |
|---|---|---|---|---|---|---|---|---|
| *Hilly Region* | | | | | | | | |
| Pansa | 3.8 | 2.3 | 7.3 | 1.9 | - | - | - | 15.3 |
| Sembalpani | 7.1 | 7.0 | 11.6 | 2.3 | 70.0 | 2.9 | 3.7 | 104.6 |
| Sub total | 5.5 | 4.7 | 9.5 | 2.1 | 35.0 | 1.5 | 1.9 | 59.9 |
| *Plain Region* | | | | | | | | |
| Mahuda | 2.3 | 1.8 | 4.2 | 2.5 | - | - | - | 11.0 |
| Sandhosi | 1.7 | 1.4 | 4.3 | 1.9 | 3.0 | 2.4 | 2.2 | 16.9 |
| Sub total | 1.8 | 1.5 | 4.3 | 2.0 | 2.5 | 2.0 | 2.0 | 16.0 |

*Source*: Field Survey, 1985-86.

TABLE 7.16: **Production and sale of milk, ghee and farmyard mannure**

*(Monthly average per household)*

| *Sample village* | *Quantity of milk produced (in litres)* | *Percen-tage if sold* | *Quantity of ghee sold (in Rs.)* | *Percen-tage if sold* | *FYM quantity produced (in Rs.)* | *Percen-tage if sold* |
|---|---|---|---|---|---|---|
| *Hilly Region* | | | | | | |
| Pansa | 58.2(19.4) | 33.3 | 1.6(0.7) | 43.8 | 190.6 | 0.0 |
| Sembalpani | 122.7(94.0) | 76.6 | 1.8(1.8) | 100.0 | 518.7 | 92.7 |
| Sub total | 90.5(56.7) | 62.7 | 1.7(1.2) | 70.6 | 354.6 | 67.8 |
| *Plain Region* | | | | | | |
| Mahuda | 63.0(18.0) | 28.6 | 1.9(1.0) | 52.6 | 122.0 | 0.0 |
| Sandhosi | 83.2(59.3) | 71.3 | 2.3(1.8) | 78.3 | 304.6 | 0.0 |
| Sub total | 80.2(52.0) | 64.8 | 2.3(1.6) | 69.6 | 276.9 | 0.0 |
| Total | 85.8(54.6) | 63.6 | 2.0(1.4) | 70.0 | 319.5 | 41.2 |

*Source*: Field Survey,1985-86.

Figures in brackets indicate the quantity sold.

Though the government has a scheme of tribal development under which milch animals are given, it can be seen in this case that the non-tribals in the tribal region have benefitted. Considering the activity of Rabaris it could be realised that the activity of livestock rearing has a potential of adding considerably to the household income and, also, implicitly to the household employment. It has to be made acceptable for the tribal.

**Value of assets**

An attempt is made to understand conditions of living environment in terms of the total number and value of their domestic assets. The items included for valuation are house, furniture, utensils, baskets, grain drums, farm implements, musical instruments and others. The average value of the assets is higher (Rs. 8,081) in the households of sample village in the plain region than the sample villages in the hilly region (Rs. 6,212). Among the 4 sample villages the households of Sandhosi village have relatively valuable assets (Rs. 8,119) and households of Pansa village have assets of lesser value (Rs. 5,483) as shown in Table 7.17.

Out of the total average value of household assets in these four sample villages, nearly 87 per cent is in the form of house. Houses in the plains are more expensive than those in the hilly region. Again, the difference in the value of a house is greater in the hilly region compared to the plains. Other valuable assets of sample households include farm implements (three to five per cent of total value) and household utensils three per cent of value). However, it is interesting to note that the households in the plain region have higher absolute value for almost all assets.

Thus, the persent study on the socio-cultural traits sustaining tribal ecology in a micro-region of North Gujarat brings out the following significant findings:

(a) Some of the demographic characteristics in relative terms are: High density of population (122 persons per sq. km.), female proportion (971 females per 1000 males), literacy including female literacy (5 per cent), high dependency ratio (especially female dependency ratio (1:39), large family size (8.3) and low average geographical area (550 hectares) are associated with the sample villages of the plain region.

TABLE 7.17: **Average value of household assets**

*(in Rs.)*

| *Sample Villages* | *House* | *Furniture* | *Utensils* | *Baskkets* | *Grain drum* | *Farm implements* | *Musical instruments* | *Others* | *Total* |
|---|---|---|---|---|---|---|---|---|---|
| *Hilly Region* | | | | | | | | | |
| Pansa | 4750 | 75 | 194 | 14 | 32 | 285 | 67 | 66 | 5483 |
| | (86.6) | (1.4) | (3.5) | (0.25) | (0.58) | (5.2) | (1.2) | (1.2) | (100) |
| Sembalpani | 6200 | 70 | 213 | 14 | 49 | 248 | 67 | 79 | 6940 |
| | (89.3) | (1.0) | (3.1) | (0.20) | (0.71) | (3.6) | (0.96) | (1.1) | (100) |
| Sub total | 5475 | 73 | 204 | 28 | 41 | 267 | 67 | 73 | 6212 |
| | (88.1) | (1.2) | (3.3) | (0.45) | (0.66) | (4.3) | (1.1) | (1.2) | (100) |
| *Plain Region* | | | | | | | | | |
| Mahuda | 6800 | 210 | 210 | 31 | 68 | 384 | 83 | 81 | 7867 |
| | (86.4) | (2.7) | (2.7) | (0.39) | (0.86) | (4.9) | (1.1) | (1.0) | (100) |
| Sandhosi | 7036 | 115 | 279 | 33 | 37 | 269 | 69 | 281 | 8119 |
| | (86.7) | (1.4) | (3.4) | (0.41) | (0.45) | (3.3) | (0.85) | (3.5) | (100) |
| Sub total | 7000 | 129 | 269 | 33 | 42 | 286 | 33 | 251 | 8081 |
| | (86.6) | (1.6) | (3.3) | (0.41) | (0.52) | (3.5) | (0.41) | (3.1) | (100) |
| Total | 6164 | 98 | 233 | 22 | 41 | 276 | 69 | 153 | 7057 |
| | (87.3) | (1.4) | (3.3) | (0.31) | (0.86) | (3.9) | (0.98) | (2.2) | (100) |

*Source*: Field Survey, 1985-86.
Figures in bracket show percentage

(b) The participation of women in subsidiary occupation is greater (65 per cent) than the participation of men (35 per cent) and more so in the sample villages of plain region (female participation -71 per cent).

(c) The average duration and distance of migration from the sample villages of hilly region is shorter (duration 6 months and distance 20 kms) than that of the villages of plain region (average duration 10 months and distance 75 kms).

(d) The sample households of plain region interact (economic purpose) with more settlements (seven in number) than the households of hilly region (two in number).

(e) The per household annual income is higher in the villages of plain region (Rs. 6,065) than in the villages of hilly region (Rs. 4,950).

(f) The major sources of household income in the sample villages of hilly region are forest (33 per cent) and animal products (33 per cent) and in case of plain region are agricultural (49 per cent) and animal products (26 per cent).

(g) The average number of livestock population per household is higher in the villages of hilly region (60 in number including all types of livestock) than the villages of plain region (16 in number).

(h) The average per ha. cost of agricultural production (including seed, fertiliser and irrigation cost) is higher in the sample villages of hilly region (Rs. 795) than in the sample villages of plain region (Rs. 740). It is interesting to note the deviation that the per hectare agricultural production is higher in the villages of hilly region (917 kg. per hectare) - mainly because of the high yield per hectare in the agricultural holdings which are under concealed ownership or tenancy than in the villages of plain region (617 kg. per hectare).

(i) The average quantity of milk produced and sold in the villages of hilly region is higher (93 litres and 63 litres) than in the villages of plain region (80 litres and 65 litres).

(j) The average value of assets (house, furniture, utensils, baskets, grain drums, farm implements, etc.) per household in the villages of hilly region is lower (Rs. 6,210) than in the households of villages in the plain region (Rs. 8,080).

(k) As mentioned earlier the food items and building materials of the tribal households are dependent on the resources derived from the forests, animals and agriculture.

The preceding analysis, thus, highlights various demographic, social and economic characteristics of the sample households of this micro-region and brings out distinct patterns in their micro-geographical regions (hilly and plain). These micro-environments have significantly influenced the households. The direct and indirect influence of micro-environment is reflected in the size of household, density, dependency, livelihood, sources and levels of income, movement patterns, land-use, agricultural production, cropping pattern, food habits and housing material in these sample villages.

It is also pertinent to note that the tribals, who had inherited rich forest and had adjusted their life patterns on this resource base are now finding it more and more difficult to sustain it. On the one hand, their population has increased. On the other, demands on forest resources have also mounted because of forces of the economy in general. Both these factors have led to degradation of forest resources.

Tribals on their part have not taken to other occupations in any way. Lack of education has hindered their occupational capability. It has also kept them away from any system of communication which can usher in modernisation. Though government efforts keep these ideas as goals or objective as per the situation the expected impact of the ITDP programme has yet to be found.

## NOTES

1. The lower female proportion in the sample villages of hilly region (according to the Census) may be due to the presence of males who did not migrate during census enumeration (average six months a year).
2. Low altitude with less undulations, better soil (sandy loamy soil) and water availability.
3. Accessibility (TPT) Communication, more interaction, diffusion of innovation and scope for the use of modern implements.

# 8

# CONCLUSIONS AND RECOMMENDATIONS

THIS PILOT study reveals that the whole tribal life is woven together in a remarkable way with the forest. Since they are habitual dwellers of the forest area they have learnt to rely on the forest resources for their traditional living pattern. It is found that the relationship of tribals with forest has not changed much in spite of all the developmental efforts undertaken so far. This is mainly because the stance of development programmes has not been intune with their traditional way of resource use.

The tribals, as examined in this report, rely on forests for meeting their needs of material for housing, agricultural implements, herbal medicine, etc. Forest for them are also store houses for fodder and fuelwood. The activity of collecting MFP also provides them with employment opportunities.

However, because of number of reasons including the increasing population pressure, both within and outside the tribal areas, the forest wealth is being over-exploited. The all-round over-exploitation has caused serious shortfall in the supply of forest based items which used to meet various needs of the tribals. As the traditional tribal life is interwoven with forest, over-exploitation of forest is causing a serious socio-cultural dislocation almost in the same proportion of its reliance on forest wealth.

Loss of forest cover has many environmental consequences. The depletion of soil fertility, deepening of acquifers, increased rate of run-off, disfunctionality of the traditional saran system of irrigation on slopes, loss of birds and game causing loss of animal protein, etc., can be enumerated. The matter becomes equally serious as some particular specie becomes extinct or near extinct. Bamboo is a case in point. The Garasias of Sandhosi village, for example, no longer put up a bamboo fence around the courtyard. They are, thus, deprived of kepping poultry also, as they could not be protected against carnivorous animals.

Bamboo is also used for the construction of houses in walls, ceilings, etc. It will be neither financially possible to replace bamboo by modern materials, such as iron, cement-concrete, bricks, etc., nor will it be culturally satisfying.

## Forest species and their uses

The forests in Danta taluka are non-teak, dry deciduous, scrub type. The top level is comprised of about 15 dominant varieties and 16 less dominant varieties which attain a height of more than eight metres. The middle level consists of 20 major species growing to a height between two and eight metres. At the ground level there are four dominant species and another nine are less dominant. Thus, the forest has a good diversity as nearly 45 species grow here in natural conditions.

The tribals have shown great adaptability to the environment around them. The species are put to uses like fuelwood, timber and farm implements. Wood is also used in construction of houses and a large variety is put to medicinal and other uses. The medicinal uses need a special reference as these uses are determined by cumulative traditional wisdom of generations. The traditional method of learning these uses are transferred from fathers to sons. The transfer is from one generation to another, where word of mouth is the method of communication. Since the rate of literacy is very low the information is kept only in the oral tradition. Neither are the uses properly chronicled nor are all the processes, which are involved, properly documented by the outside world. It is a matter of great concern that this accumulated knowledge will gradually disappear with the extinction of specific species from the forests. The tribals will be deprived of their traditional system while the new and the modern system will not be reaching them considering the present stance of development. The resultant dislocation can only be imagined.

Indeed the tribals have taken up settled crop-cultivation since long and, hence, it would be an exaggeration to believe that their economic system revolves around forests only. Yet, the tribals have exhibited an adaptive relationship with forests which has a long and watchful history of a chain of trial and error at the back of it. This chain has culminated into an essence of functional wisdom which is specific to their situation.

## Forests and economic interaction

Forest supports economic interaction of the tribals with outside world. Though, the tribals are inward oriented, on certain counts they are required to come into contact with the non-tribal world through exchange. The practice of mixed cropping serves a dual function. For example, as a maize-groundnut or maize-cotton mix, on the one hand, it meets the subsistence needs; on the other, the commercial crop, viz., groundnut or cotton provides easy marketability. Through the process of sale of many similar products which are based both on forests and agriculture, like, honey, dholi or kali musli, gugal, etc., (all MFP), animal products like ghee and milk and commercial crops, the tribals try to meet their cash requirements which arises mainly from purchase of inputs and requirement of social services.

In this interaction forests have an important role to play. Forests are grazing ground for livestock. Fuelwood, bamboo and MFP collected from the forest are sold to outside world for which a ready market exists. In the process, forest provides an easy and socially acceptable avenue for employment, which, in such a micro-region, has to be from the primary sectors of production. However, since the forests are degraded, their economic base has also shrunk. Simultaneously, their agriculture has not grown in a compensatory way. Hence, the depletion of forest is directly related with the weakening of their economic base. Any thoughtful programme of tribal development ought to take this aspect into proper prospective.

## Life patterns in hilly and plain regions

The hilly region has a larger proportion of land under non-arable and forest categories which is due to obvious reasons. This prevailing pattern of land-use affects the tribals' way of living in a significant way as they determine their major economic activities.

The second important aspect of crop productivity is that the yield rate in plains is lesser than that of in the hilly region. The difference is difficult to explain as it would be generally expected that the plain region should have a higher level of productivity. However, such disturbance can be explained by the fact that in village Sembalpani, output of wheat is reported to be rather too high. When juxtaposed with the average cost of inputs, one can see that it is not very high in case of hilly regions as compared to the plains.

It is also observed that the households in plain regions have greater interaction with the outside world in comparison with those in hilly regions which also is to be expected.

Next, the households in hilly region have larger size of herd as compared to those in the plain regions. This is to be expected as the hilly region has larger land sizes under non-arable and forest areas.

As a result of better infrastructural and other facilities, better methods of crop cultivation, etc., the average value of assets held by a household in plain region is much larger than that held in a hilly region.

## Recommendations

The analysis of statistical and other qualitative information collected under this pilot study of this micro-region, viz., Danta taluka, suggests the following two areas for further study and policy action:

(a) **Areas for Further Study**

The preliminary findings of this study show that the tribals rely heavily on forests to meet their felt needs for housing materials, timber, agricultural implements, medicine, etc. However, in order to gain better insight into this, in depth studies in the following areas are suggested:

(i) *Quantification of various forest-based needs*: All forest based needs should be quantified and the requirement of forest resources in relation to the size of population should be worked out in detail by each item.

(ii) *Reinforcement of cultural traits of tribals*: The tribals derive greater cultural satisfaction from hunting, collecting MFP and thus getting additional income (in kind) from roaming in forests. Because of their traditional pride derived from the Rajput lineage they would love to have denser and more productive forests. Because of their age old wisdom of herbal medicine they would like to have a diversified flora. Needs like those originating from housing and agriculture and animal husbandry also require a greater diversification of species. These and other similar cultural traits should be consciously reinforced and the tribals should be encouraged to undertake such plantations.

(iii) *Consumption of Mahuda flowers*: Mahuda flowers are an important item of MFP. It is essential to know the exact pattern of Mahuda flower consumption among the tribals.

(iv) *Consumption of Doli*: Mahuda seed (Doli)is the main oilseed in this region. A study may be conducted to know the consumption pattern of Doli oil in this tribal area and its effect on the human wealth.

(v) *Study of effects of cultural practices on gum yielding trees*: The gum yielding trees may react differently to treatments like watering, manuring, soil working, etc., during tapping season. If their reaction is favourable, from the point of view of its quantity and quality it would be advisable to practise the best treatment in the yield too. It is, therefore, recommended that a study on the effect of watering, soil working, manuring, etc., on the gum yielding trees may be conducted.

(vi) *Study of Timru leaves for raising quality level*: Timru is one of the important trees. However, it is seen that all the leaves are not collected by the tribal as most of the leaves are damaged and defoliated either due to fungus attack or due to insect attack. By a rough reconking more than 60 per cent of the leaves are damaged in this way. It is, therefore, essential to devise ways and means to control the insect and fungus damage in timru leaves.

(vii) *Standardisation of Timru leaves:* The leaves of Timru plant vary much in size and shape. The quality of leaves depend upon the size, shape, thickness, pliability, colour, etc., of the leaves. All best characteristics are found in certain clonal varieties of Timru. It is, therefore, essential to identify the clonal variety with the best characteristic and then propogate the same on an extensive scale.

(viii) *Inclusion of MFP species in SFP:* There are certain MFP plants available in this region, namely, Chilni Bhaji (*chlorofyfum tuberosum*) and safed musli. Due to the depletion of natural resources, the production of such MFP is declining day-by-day. Therefore, it is very essential to propagate this specie artificially in this tribal tract. However, authentic information about their cultivation not forthcomming. Thus, it may be worthwhile to find out the foolproof techniques of raising this plant artificially. Hence, it is recommended that efforts should be made to evolve foolproof techniques of raising the plantation of this specie artificially.

(ix) *Study of gum yielding species:* There are many gum yielding plants in this region, namely *Steculis ureus* (Kadaya) and *Bosevellea Serrata* (Salai). The tribals earn quite a sizable amount of wages through the collection of these gums. There are certain methods in vogue wherein some chemicals are used in tapping to get a good quantity of gum, but with injurious results sometimes. Therefore, it is essential to know the best tapping method and best chemical to be used to get increased output of gum without causing a serious injury to the plant.

(x) *Harvesting of Gugal:* Ethylene, a plant growth regulator has been used to increase resin exudates. The forest department should employ this method to boost up 'Gugal' production.

(xi) *Afforestation for oil extraction:* Our country is experiencing acute shortage of oils. The attention is now being focussed forwards unconventional oil sources and trees of forest areas with oilseeds are gaining ground. In this forest area, there are many trees which can give us oilseeds in considerable quantity, but their seeds are not collected due to various reasons. It is essential to explore the possibility of collecting unconventional oilseeds from this forest area in maximum quantity. Therefore, it is recommended to take up the exploratory survey of oilseeds of forest origin and organize the collection. Along with this study of neem-seed oil is also recommended.

(xii) *Raising forest as common property resources:* The tribals have a higher degree of fraternity than that of non-tribals. Their system of working on each other's farms without cash wage payment and not fragmenting land among all brothers at father's death are cases in point. This trait can be utilised by making a whole village partner in sharing benefits of an adjoining forest area. The villagers can decide their needs and plantation can become need based. It could be successfully raised provided they are also helped in proper management of it.

(xii) *Role of tribal women in raising forest:* The tribal women, along with men and children are observed working in forests not only to meet their felt household needs but also to supplement the household income. Such cash income is required to meet the monetized part of their need. The women power, in this way, is also related with forest and can be made to participate fruitfully in raising forests. This part should be analysed from the socio-economic angle in order to find out a basis of their involvement.

Very little of the wealth extracted from the forests filters down to and remains in the tribal communities. It is no wonder, therefore, that tribals find very little motivation to support government forestry prevailing conservation and restoration programmes. In this situation, the forest property has been damaged to a great extent. There exists a credibility gap which is too injurious. Credibility must be restored first. Tribal must trust government. This can happen once the tribals realise that their history, culture and traditions are an important inputs in economic development.

### (b) Policy Recommendations

As it is observed that the tribals have evinced a very close reliance on forests some policy recommendations also emerge from this:

(i) *Share in Management and Profits:* Tribals economy should be supported by forest management innovations, such as, sharing in management and profits.

(ii) *Buffer forests*: The tribals exploit forests for their personal uses. However, the pressure on forests keeps on mounting as the forests become scarcer. In order to save the diversified and rich flora and fauna, some additional forest areas should be earmarked as buffers for their exploitation. This can save the remaining forest area. Such buffers should be carefully worked out and monitored as part of a sustainable management plan. However, euvigourating the forests should be the first step in the right direction.

(iii) *Broader management view of the forest resources:* Policy implications of a broader management view of the forest resource-base should be a part of forest development policy for the tribals. The contours of such a policy view-point are very important. For example, the output required from these forests should form an integral part of the State policy of managing its forest resources. Thus, the required quantity of MFP, timber, etc., to meet both local and regional needs should be worked out with a view to both temporal and spatial dimensions. This will require a detailed study of item-wise need of forest produce. Supply of each of these items, ideally, should form the basis of the plantation programme. While doing this, a gradual transition away from forest resource use should be introduced. Spread of literacy, better farming practices, better means and methods of forest exploitation, etc., can provide a better chance of regeneration of forests.

(iv) *Tribal Co-operatives for MFP:* It is desirable to establish small co-operative of tribal people who are the primary collectors of MFP and entrust the work to them only.

(v) *Assuring the possible returns:* The tribals are not very good at managing their affairs at the markets. Bacause of relatively secluded nature of their living they are not well-informed on the count of market phenomena. Thus, in order to earn the required amount of income to meet their cash needs, they have to sell larger quantities, say, of the MFP. This process has disastrous impact on forests. Besides, tribals, whose interests are co-terminus with the forests, are required to go against their own long-term interest.

A proper system of marketing organised as a tribals cartel or holding company should work as a counter-vailing power against the monopolistic behaviour of traders. Tribal youth should be trained in various crafts based on forest product. They should be also given education and practical training in various aspects of development.

(vi) *Use of Marginal Lands:* Marginal lands should be put under afforestation and sociai forestry programme

(vii) *Processing of value addition:* The tribal generally sell-off the forest produce in the form of a raw material. They should be provided with skills, technology and all necessary inputs and infrastructure to convert the raw materials into semi-finished or finished goods. The following brief list gives a suggestive outline.

| *The Raw Materials* | *Value Added product* |
|---|---|
| Tendu leaves | Bidi |
| Khakhra leaves | Padiya, Paatrala |
| Khakhra root | Extraction |
| Hardc, Behda, Ambla | Trifala powder and tablets also Harde powder and tablets as Ayurvedic medicine |
| Gugal | Incense sticks |
| Fuel wood | Billets, charcoal |
| Timber | Sizes, Furniture |

The rich diversity of flora of this area can, in this way, enable the tribals lead a more developed life as they can have more assured income and employment. This pattern of development shall be more meaningful as the tribals shall have the developmental approach which will be culturally most satisfying.

(viii) *Tribal Literacy and Afforestation:* Tribal youth should be trained in various crafts based an forest products. They should also be given education and practical training in various aspects of development. Forestry programmes must be carried out like a movement with the active involvement of tribals at all levels.

TABLE 1.1: **Some Aspects of production and consumption of the Tribal Households**

*(Pansa)*

| *Land size* | *Name of crop* | *Av.pro duct per hh (in kg)* | *Av.pur- chase per hh (in kg)* | *Total (A)* | *Av.cons. per hh (in kg) (B)* | *Netmar- ket able surplus (A-B)* | *Market -ed surp- lus* | *Av.cons percent per day (in kg)* |
|---|---|---|---|---|---|---|---|---|
| 0.01-1.00 | Maize | 153.333 | 177.857 | 331.190 | 153.333 | 177.857 | - | 0.070 |
| | Wheat | 833.571 | 116.667 | 955.238 | 958.393 | 113.095 | 130.000 | 0.438 |
| | Ragi | 105.000 | 10.000 | 115.000 | 20.000 | 90.000 | 90.000 | 0.009 |
| | Udad | 40.000 | - | 40.000 | 6.667 | 33.333 | 23.000 | 0.003 |
| | Tur | 39.000 | - | 39.000 | 5.000 | 34.000 | 49.000 | 0.002 |
| | Chola | 31.250 | - | 31.250 | 5.000 | 26.250 | 32.500 | 0.002 |
| | Gram | 400.000 | - | 400.000 | 20.000 | 380.000 | 80.000 | 0.009 |
| 1.01-2.00 | Maize | 122.857 | 296.667 | 419.524 | 122.857 | 296.667 | - | 0.056 |
| | Wheat | 593.333 | - | 593.333 | 526.667 | 66.666 | 200.000 | 0.240 |
| | Ragi | 120.000 | - | 120.000 | - | 120.000 | 125.000 | - |
| | Udad | 40.000 | - | 40.000 | 40.000 | - | - | 0.018 |
| | Tur | 120.000 | - | 120.000 | 5.000 | 115.000 | 117.500 | 0.002 |
| | Chola | - | - | - | - | - | - | - |
| | Gram | 20.000 | 2.000 | 22.000 | - | 22.000 | 20.000 | - |
| | Caster seed | 20.000 | 1.000 | 21.000 | - | 21.000 | 20.000 | - |
| | Cotton | 80.000 | - | - | - | 80.000 | 40.000 | - |
| 2.01-4.00 | Maize | 380.000 | 300.000 | 680.000 | 213.000 | 467.000 | - | 0.065 |
| | Wheat | 1100.000 | 100.000 | 1200.000 | 600.000 | 600.000 | 800.000 | 0.183 |
| | Ragi | 300.000 | 6.000 | 306.000 | - | 306.000 | 300.000 | - |
| | Udad | 73.333 | - | 73.333 | 12.500 | 60.833 | 73.333 | 0.004 |
| | Tur | 122.500 | 3.500 | 126.000 | 12.500 | 113.500 | 110.000 | 0.004 |
| | Chola | 20.000 | - | 20.000 | 60.000 | 40.000 | 15.000 | 0.018 |
| | Gram | 150.00 | - | 150.000 | 5.000 | 145.000 | 180.000 | 0.002 |
| Total | Maize | 177.895 | 227.917 | 405.812 | 151.579 | 254.233 | - | 0.059 |
| | Wheat | 820.833 | 112.500 | 933.333 | 793.000 | 140.333 | 412.000 | 0.310 |
| | Ragi | 137.143 | 8.000 | 145.143 | 20.000 | 125.143 | 143.333 | 0.008 |
| | Udad | 54.286 | - | 54.286 | 14.667 | 39.619 | 48.333 | 0.006 |
| | Tur | 75.556 | - | 75.556 | 7.500 | 68.056 | 77.778 | 0.003 |
| | Chola | 29.000 | - | 29.000 | 27.000 | 2.000 | 26.667 | 0.011 |
| | Gram | 180.000 | 2.000 | 182.000 | 12.500 | 169.500 | 93.333 | 0.005 |
| | Caster seed | 21.000 | 21.000 | 21.000 | - | 21.000 | 60.000 | - |
| | Cotton | 80.000 | - | 80.000 | - | 80.000 | 40.000 | - |

*Source*: Field Survey.

TABLE 1.2: **Some Asppects of production and consumption of the Tribal Households**
*(Sambalpani)*

| *Land size* | *Name of crop* | *Av.pro-duct per hh (in kg)* | *Av.pur-chase per hh (in kg)* | *Total (A)* | *Av.cons. per hh (in kg) (B)* | *Netmar-ketable surplus (A-B)* | *Market-ed surp-lus* | *Av.cons percent per day (in kg)* |
|---|---|---|---|---|---|---|---|---|
| 0.01-1.00 | Maize | 120.000 | - | 120.000 | 120.000 | - | - | 0.019 |
| | Udad | 20.000 | - | 20.000 | - | 20.000 | 20.000 | - |
| | Til | 40.000 | - | 40.000 | - | 40.000 | 40.000 | - |
| | Kalathi | 40.000 | - | 40.000 | - | 40.000 | 40.000 | - |
| 1.01-2.00 | Maize | 100.000 | - | 100.000 | 100.000 | - | - | 0.039 |
| | Wheat | 100.000 | - | 100.000 | 100.000 | - | - | 0.039 |
| | Udad | 30.000 | - | 30.000 | 30.000 | - | - | 0.012 |
| | Chola | 40.000 | - | 40.000 | 20.000 | 20.000 | 20.000 | 0.008 |
| | Kalathi | 30.000 | - | 30.000 | 15.000 | 15.000 | 15.000 | 0.006 |
| | Gram | 20.000 | - | 20.000 | - | 20.000 | 20.000 | - |
| 2.01-4.00 | Maize | 120.000 | - | 120.000 | 120.000 | - | - | 0.047 |
| | Wheat | 1000.000 | - | 1000.000 | 100.000 | 900.000 | - | 0.039 |
| | Udad | 20.000 | - | 20.000 | - | 20.000 | 20.000 | - |
| | Chola | 20.000 | - | 20.000 | - | 20.000 | 20.000 | - |
| 4.01 + | Maize | 500.000 | - | 500.000 | 500.000 | - | - | 0.274 |
| | Wheat | 1000.000 | - | 1000.000 | 1000.000 | - | - | 0.548 |
| | Chola | 10.000 | - | 10.000 | 10.000 | - | - | 0.005 |
| Total | Maize | 188.000 | - | 188.000 | 194.000 | 6.000 | - | 0.059 |
| | Wheat | 700.000 | - | 700.000 | 700.000 | - | - | 0.213 |
| | Udad | 25.000 | - | 25.000 | 30.000 | 5.000 | 20.000 | 0.009 |
| | Til | 40.000 | - | 40.000 | - | 40.000 | 40.000 | - |
| | Kalathi | 33.333 | - | 33.333 | 15.000 | 18.333 | 23.333 | 0.005 |
| | Gram | 20.000 | - | 20.000 | - | 20.000 | 20.000 | - |
| | Chola | 23.333 | - | 23.333 | 15.000 | 8.333 | 20.000 | 0.005 |

*Source*: Field Survey.

TABLE 1.3: **Some Aspects of production and consumption of the Tribal Households**

*(Mahuda)*

| *Land size* | *Name of crop* | *Av.pro-duct per hh (in kg)* | *Av.pur-chase per hh (in kg)* | *Total (A)* | *Av.cons. per hh (in kg) (B)* | *Netmar-ketable surplus (A-B)* | *Market -ed surp-lus* | *Av.cons percent per day (in kg)* |
|---|---|---|---|---|---|---|---|---|
| 0.01-1.00 | Maize | 100.000 | - | 100.000 | 100.000 | - | - | 0.030 |
| | Udad | 50.000 | - | 50.000 | 10.000 | 40.000 | 40.000 | 0.003 |
| | Tur | 100.000 | - | 100.000 | 10.000 | 90.000 | 90.000 | 0.003 |
| 1.01-2.00 | Maize | 70.000 | 400.000 | 470.000 | 70.000 | 400.000 | - | 0.038 |
| | Wheat | 300.000 | 200.000 | 500.000 | 100.000 | 400.000 | 200.000 | 0.055 |
| 2.01-4.00 | Maize | 250.000 | - | 250.000 | 250.000 | - | - | 0.045 |
| | Wheat | 300.000 | - | 300.000 | 300.000 | - | - | 0.059 |
| | Cotton | 250.000 | - | 250.000 | - | 250.000 | 250.000 | - |
| | Chola | 40.000 | - | 40.000 | - | 40.000 | - | - |
| | Tur | 200.000 | - | 200.000 | - | 200.000 | - | - |
| 4.01 + | Maize | 300.000 | 140.000 | 440.000 | 300.000 | 140.000 | - | 0.051 |
| | Wheat | 400.000 | - | 400.000 | 200.000 | 200.000 | - | 0.034 |
| | Udad | 40.000 | - | 40.000 | 10.000 | 30.000 | 30.000 | 0.002 |
| | Tur | 40.000 | - | 40.000 | 10.000 | 30.000 | 30.000 | 0.002 |
| | Cotton | 100.000 | - | 100.000 | - | 100.000 | 100.000 | - |
| Total | Maize | 194.000 | 270.000 | 464.000 | 194.000 | 270.000 | - | 0.048 |
| | Wheat | 333.333 | 200.000 | 533.333 | 200.000 | 233.333 | 200.000 | 0.050 |
| | Udad | 45.000 | - | 45.000 | 10.000 | 35.000 | 35.000 | 0.002 |
| | Tur | 113.333 | - | 113.333 | 10.000 | 103.333 | 160.000 | 0.002 |
| | Cotton | 200.000 | - | 200.000 | - | 200.000 | 175.000 | - |
| | Chola | 40.000 | - | 40.000 | - | 40.000 | 20.000 | - |

*Source*: Field survey.

TABLE 1.4: **Some Aspects of production and consumption of the Tribal Households**

*(Sandhosi)*

| *Land size* | *Name of crop* | *Av.pro-duct per hh (in kg)* | *Av.pur-chase per hh (in kg)* | *Total (A)* | *Av.cons. per hh (in kg) (B)* | *Netmar-ketable surplus (A-B)* | *Market -ed surp-lus* | *Av.cons percent pe day (in kg)* |
|---|---|---|---|---|---|---|---|---|
| 0.01-1.00 | Maize | 234.545 | 60.000 | 294.000 | 234.545 | 60.545 | - | 0.080 |
| | Wheat | 506.667 | 20.000 | 526.000 | 360.000 | 246.000 | 600.000 | 0.123 |
| | Udad | 53.333 | - | 53.333 | 25.286 | 28.047 | 44.778 | 0.009 |
| | Gram | 120.000 | - | 120.000 | 13.333 | 106.667 | 106.667 | 0.005 |
| | Tur | 81.111 | - | 81.111 | 15.000 | 66.111 | 67.778 | 0.005 |
| | Cotton | 205.455 | - | 205.455 | - | 205.455 | 205.455 | - |
| | Garlic | 10.000 | - | 10.000 | - | 10.000 | 10.000 | - |
| 1.01-2.00 | Maize | 485.000 | 20.000 | 505.000 | 485.000 | 20.000 | 800.000 | 0.190 |
| | Wheat | 716.667 | 30.000 | 746.000 | 700.000 | 46.000 | - | 0.274 |
| | Udad | 125.000 | 2.000 | 127.000 | 13.333 | 113.667 | 81.571 | 0.005 |
| | Tur | 90.000 | 3.000 | 93.000 | 10.000 | 83.000 | 63.143 | 0.004 |
| | Gram | 465.000 | - | 465.000 | 486.667 | 21.667 | 90.000 | 0.190 |
| | Cotton | 362.500 | 1.000 | 363.500 | - | 363.500 | 282.500 | - |
| | Rice | 450.000 | - | 450.000 | 300.000 | 150.000 | - | 0.117 |
| 2.01-4.00 | Maize | 300.000 | - | 300.000 | 280.000 | 20.000 | 5.000 | 0.128 |
| | Wheat | 366.667 | - | 366.667 | 366.667 | - | 5.000 | 0.167 |
| | Udad | 72.500 | 2.000 | 74.500 | - | 74.500 | 55.000 | - |
| | Tur | 126.667 | - | 126.667 | - | 126.667 | 122.500 | - |
| | Gram | 80.000 | 60.000 | 140.000 | 80.000 | 160.000 | - | 0.037 |
| | Cotton | 573.333 | - | 573.333 | - | 573.333 | 609.500 | - |
| 4.01 + | Maize | 560.000 | - | 560.000 | 506.667 | 53.333 | 20.000 | 0.116 |
| | Wheat | 500.000 | - | 500.000 | 450.000 | 50.000 | - | 0.103 |
| | Gram | 240.000 | - | 240.000 | 240.000 | - | 20.000 | 0.055 |
| | Cotton | 330.000 | 3.000 | 333.000 | - | 333.000 | 260.000 | - |
| | Rice | 60.000 | - | 60.000 | 60.000 | - | - | - |
| | Udad | 20.000 | - | 20.000 | - | 20.000 | 20.000 | 0.014 |
| | Tur | 20.000 | - | 20.000 | - | 20.000 | 20.000 | - |
| Total | Maize | 361.111 | 50.000 | 411.111 | 359.643 | 51.468 | 275.000 | 0.123 |
| | Wheat | 555.294 | 25.000 | 580.294 | 500.000 | 80.294 | 401.667 | 0.171 |
| | Udad | 84.286 | 2.000 | 86.286 | 19.769 | 66.517 | 58.105 | 0.007 |
| | Tur | 91.667 | 3.000 | 94.667 | 13.364 | 181.308 | 69.316 | 0.005 |
| | Gram | 282.222 | 60.000 | 342.222 | 227.500 | 114.722 | 86.000 | 0.078 |
| | Cotton | 327.826 | 2.000 | 329.826 | - | 329.826 | 269.947 | - |
| | Rice | 320.000 | - | 320.000 | 180.000 | 140.000 | - | 0.062 |
| | Garlic | 10.000 | - | 10.000 | - | 10.000 | 10.000 | - |

*Source*: Field Survey.

TABLE 1.5: **Some Aspects of production and consumption of the Tribal Households**

*(All Four Sample Villages)*

| *Land size* | *Name of crop* | *Av.product per hh (in kg)* | *Av.purchase per hh (in kg)* | *Total (A)* | *Av.cons. per hh (in kg) (B)* | *Netmarketable surplus (A-B)* | *Marketed surplus* | *Av.cons percent per day (in kg)* |
|---|---|---|---|---|---|---|---|---|
| 0.01-1.00 | Maize | 190.000 | 142.700 | 332.700 | 190.000 | 142.700 | - | 0.065 |
| | Wheat | 685.385 | 92.500 | 777.885 | 684.364 | 93.521 | 365.000 | 0.234 |
| | Ragi | 105.000 | 10.000 | 115.000 | 20.000 | 95.000 | 90.000 | 0.007 |
| | Udad | 47.857 | - | 47.857 | 18.818 | 29.039 | 39.071 | 0.006 |
| | Tur | 68.333 | - | 68.333 | 12.083 | 56.250 | 43.000 | 0.004 |
| | Chola | 125.000 | - | 125.000 | 5.000 | 120.000 | 32.000 | 0.002 |
| | Gram | 190.000 | - | 190.000 | 215.000 | 175.000 | 42.000 | 0.005 |
| | Cotton | 205.000 | - | 205.000 | - | 205.000 | 205.000 | - |
| | Kalathi | 40.000 | - | 40.000 | - | 40.000 | 40.000 | - |
| | Til | 40.000 | - | 40.000 | - | 40.000 | 40.000 | - |
| | Garlic | 10.000 | - | 10.000 | - | 10.000 | 10.000 | - |
| | Rice | - | - | - | 60.000 | 60.000 | - | 0.021 |
| 1.01-2.00 | Maize | 299.00 | 262.000 | 561.000 | 299.000 | 262.000 | 800.000 | 0.117 |
| | Wheat | 589.091 | 115.000 | 704.091 | 543.636 | 160.455 | 200.000 | 0.213 |
| | Ragi | 120.000 | - | 120.000 | - | 120.000 | 200.000 | - |
| | Udad | 100.000 | 2.000 | 102.000 | 20.000 | 82.000 | 81.571 | 0.008 |
| | Tur | 97.500 | 3.000 | 100.500 | 8.750 | 91.750 | 75.222 | 0.003 |
| | Chola | 40.000 | - | 40.000 | 20.000 | 20.000 | 20.000 | 0.008 |
| | Gram | 316.667 | 2.000 | 318.667 | 486.667 | 168.000 | 43.333 | 0.190 |
| | Cotton | 306.000 | 1.000 | 307.000 | - | 307.000 | 292.500 | - |
| | Kalathi | 30.000 | - | 30.000 | 15.000 | 15.000 | 30.000 | 0.006 |
| | Rice | 450.000 | - | 450.000 | 300.000 | 150.000 | - | 0.117 |
| | Castor-seed | 20.000 | 1.000 | 21.000 | - | 21.000 | 60.000 | - |
| 2.01-4.00 | Maize | 296.000 | 300.000 | 596.000 | 238.000 | 358.000 | 5.000 | 0.082 |
| | Wheat | 657.143 | 100.000 | 757.143 | 500.000 | 257.143 | 535.143 | 0.171 |
| | Udad | 300.000 | 2.000 | 302.000 | 12.500 | 89.500 | 75.000 | 0.004 |
| | Tur | 66.250 | 3.500 | 69.750 | 12.500 | 57.250 | 232.500 | 0.004 |
| | Chola | 137.500 | - | 137.500 | 60.000 | 77.500 | 17.500 | 0.021 |
| | Gram | 26.667 | 60.000 | 86.667 | 42.500 | 44.167 | 180.000 | 0.015 |
| | Cotton | 126.667 | - | 126.667 | - | 126.667 | 489.667 | - |
| | Rice | 444.000 | - | 444.000 | - | 444.000 | - | - |
| | Ragi | - | 6.000 | 6.000 | - | 6.000 | 300.000 | - |
| 4.01 + | Maize | 480.000 | - | 480.000 | 464.000 | 16.000 | 20.000 | 0.116 |
| | Wheat | 600.000 | 140.000 | 740.000 | 525.000 | 215.000 | - | 0.131 |
| | Udad | 40.000 | - | 40.000 | 10.000 | 30.000 | 25.000 | 0.002 |
| | Tur | 40.000 | - | 40.000 | 10.000 | 30.000 | 25.000 | 0.002 |
| | Chola | 10.000 | - | 10.000 | 10.000 | - | - | 0.002 |
| | Gram | 240.000 | - | 240.000 | 240.000 | - | 20.000 | 0.060 |
| | Cotton | 253.333 | - | 253.333 | - | 253.333 | 206.667 | - |
| | Rice | 60.000 | - | 60.000 | 60.000 | - | - | 0.015 |

TABLE 1.5 *(contd)*

*(All Four Sample Villages)*

| *Land size* | *Name of crop* | *Av.pro-duct per hh (in kg)* | *Av.pur-chase per hh (in kg)* | *Total (A)* | *Av.cons. per hh (in kg) (B)* | *Netmar-ketable surplus (A-B)* | *Market -ed surp-lus* | *Av.cons percent per day (in kg)* |
|---|---|---|---|---|---|---|---|---|
| Total | Maize | 268.571 | 196.294 | 464.865 | 261.229 | 203.636 | 27.500 | 0.143 |
| | Wheat | 639.714 | 105.000 | 744.714 | 582.188 | 162.526 | 385.000 | 0.319 |
| | Ragi | 137.143 | 8.000 | 145.143 | 20.000 | 125.143 | 137.143 | 0.011 |
| | Udad | 68.824 | 2.000 | 70.824 | 19.182 | 51.642 | 51.143 | 1.011 |
| | Tur | 89.000 | 5.000 | 94.000 | 11.316 | 82.684 | 71.333 | 0.006 |
| | Chola | 42.500 | - | 42.500 | 23.857 | 18.684 | 71.233 | 0.006 |
| | Gram | 234.286 | 31.000 | 265.286 | 184.500 | 80.786 | 81.111 | 0.101 |
| | Kalathi | 33.333 | - | 33.333 | 15.000 | 18.333 | 35.000 | 0.008 |
| | Rice | 320.000 | - | 320.000 | 180.000 | 140.000 | - | 0.099 |
| | Cotton | 286.207 | 2.000 | 288.000 | - | 288.000 | 258.864 | - |
| | Garlic | 10.000 | - | 10.000 | - | 10.000 | 10.000 | - |
| | Castor-seed | 20.000 | 1.000 | 21.000 | - | 21.000 | 60.000 | - |
| | Til | 40.000 | - | 40.000 | - | 40.000 | 30.000 | - |

*Source*: Field Survey.

TABLE 1.6: **Consumption of Milk and Ghee by Sample Households**

*(Average daily all four villages)*

| *Land size class* | *Average daily consumption* | |
|---|---|---|
| | Milk (Lit.) | Ghee (grm.) |
| 0.01 - 1.00 | 0.96 | 0.02 |
| 1.01 - 2.00 | 0.97 | 0.03 |
| 2.01 - 4.00 | 1.67 | 0.03 |
| 4.01 + | 1.10 | 0.01 |
| Total | 1.04 | 0.02 |

*Source*: Field Survey.

TABLE 1.7: **Forest items Collected and Sold by the Tribals**

| *Forest Item-s* | *Frequency of collect-ors* | *Average age of collect-ors* | *Average time taken (per day in hours)* | *Average monthly income generated by per person(Rs)* | *Remarks* |
|---|---|---|---|---|---|
| Grass | 20 | 29.24 | 4.00 | 125.00 | Price per hesd load Av.Rs.5. |
| Gugal | 26 | 35.86 | 2.20 | 913.46 | Collection for 8 months forest, Rs.5/ per kg. |
| Honey | 19 | 31.33 | 1.98 | 110.53 | During the summer months March-April-May Rs.12/ per kg. |
| Dholi Musali | 5 | 33.40 | 4.22 | 116.00 | Available only in 'Kartik Mas'. |
| Fuel wood | 58 | 28.90 | 2.26 | 2359.48 | Going to forest twice in a day to collect - Rs.7 to 10 for 10 kgs headload |
| Bor | 4 | 32.50 | 0.19 | 32.50 | Avaliable during winter season. - sold in small baskets. Rs.2/- per basket |

*Source*: Field Survey.

TABLE 1.8: **Ownership of Livestock in Sample Villages**

| *Live stock* | *Average per household* | *Average per hactare* |
|---|---|---|
| Cows | 3.9 | 1.8 |
| Buffaloes | 2.4 | 0.8 |
| Goats | 7.2 | 2.8 |
| Bullocks | 2.0 | 0.7 |

*Source*: Field Survey.

TABLE 2.1: **Livestock Population of Banaskantha and Gujarat**

| *Live stock* | *Banaskantha* | | *Gujarat* | |
|---|---|---|---|---|
| | 1977 | 1982 | 1977 | 1982 |
| Cattle | 449847 (7.49) | 550276 (7.87) | 6005718 | 6994643 |
| Buffalo | 273482 (7.87) | 358293 (8.06) | 3473165 | 4443898 |
| Sheep | 200503 (12.60) | 288646 (12.24) | 1591633 | 2857258 |
| Goat | 342731 (11.11) | 345802 (10.49) | 3083898 | 3299352 |
| Horses & Ponies | 5367 (7.03) | 1284 (4.57) | 76398 | 28103 |
| Pigs | 1756 (5.23) | 9412 (5.61) | 33583 | 167816 |
| Camels | 15554 (27.59) | 12172 (16.19) | 56375 | 75192 |
| Other Livestock | 8784 (10.32) | 9887 (9.93) | 85107 | 99580 |
| Total Livestock | 1298024 (9.02) | 1575772 (9.02) | 14405877 | 17465[illegible]42 |

*Source*: Bureau of Economics and Statistics, Gandhinagar, GOG.

TABLE 2.2: **Demographic Features: Banaskantha and Gujarat**

| | | | *Banaskantha* | *Gujarat* |
|---|---|---|---|---|
| 1. | Population | M | 857319 | 17552640 |
| | | F | 810595 | 16533159 |
| | | T | 1667914 | 34085799 |
| 2. | Tribal Population | M | 57508 | 2453566 |
| | | F | 54428 | 2395020 |
| | | T | 111936 | 4848586 |
| 3. | Sex ratio general | | 891 | 942 |
| | Tribal | | 846 | 976 |
| 4. | Percentage of total state population | | 4.89 | 100.00 |
| 5. | Percentage of urban population | | 8.64 | 100.00 |

TABLE 2.2 *(contd.)*

| | | | *Banaskantha* | *Gujarat* |
|---|---|---|---|---|
| 6. | General literacy rate | M | 34.08 | 54.44 |
| | | F | 11.36 | 32.30 |
| | | T | 23.04 | 43.30 |
| 7. | Tribal literacy rate | M | 13.78 | 30.41 |
| | | F | 1.84 | 11.64 |
| | | T | 7.98 | 21.14 |
| 8. | Literacy rate: Other backward | M | 33.98 | 53.14 |
| | | F | 9.47 | 25.61 |
| | | T | 21.98 | 39.79 |

*Source*: Census of India, 1981.

TABLE 2.3: **Demographic Features: Danta and Banaskantha**

| | *Danta Taluka* | | | *Banaskantha District* | | |
|---|---|---|---|---|---|---|
| | *1961* | *1971* | *1981* | *1961* | *1971* | *1981* |
| Total population | 52411 | 70743 | 101845 | 996114 | 1265383 | 1667914 |
| Total male | 27221 | 36623 | 52326 | 511951 | 651949 | 857319 |
| Total female | 25190 | 34120 | 49519 | 484193 | 613434 | 810515 |
| Female per 1000 male | 925 | 932 | 946 | 946 | 941 | 945 |
| Density per $Km^2$ | 72 | 83 | 118 | 83 | 100 | 131 |
| Total area $Km^2$ | 730.6 | 857.2 | 860.4 | 12039.9 | 12702.0 | 12703.0 |
| Total No. of Villages | 187 | 186 | 184 | 1369 | 1360 | 1373 |
| No.of villages inhabited | 183 | 182 | 181 | 1359 | 1351 | 1366 |
| No.of Villages uninhabited | 4 | 4 | 3 | 10 | 9 | 7 |

*Source*: Census Reports, Govt. of India, New Delhi.

TABLE 2.4: **Number of Villages by Population Classes: Danta and Banaskantha**

| | *Danta Taluka* | | | *Banaskantha District* | | |
|---|---|---|---|---|---|---|
| | *1961* | *1971* | *1981* | *1961* | *1971* | *1981* |
| Less than 200 | 90 | 65 | 38 | 234 | 147 | 76 |
| 200 - 499 | 64 | 71 | 72 | 424 | 361 | 288 |
| 500 - 999 | 24 | 38 | 51 | 454 | 459 | 435 |
| 1000 - 1999 | 3 | 6 | - | 191 | 305 | 418 |
| 2000 - 4999 | 2 | 2 | - | 52 | 70 | 126 |
| 5000 - 9999 | - | - | - | 4 | 9 | 21 |
| 10000 and above | - | - | - | - | - | 2 |
| Total | 183 | 182 | 181 | 1359 | 1351 | 1366 |

*Source*: Census Reports, Govt. of India, New Delhi.

TABLE 2.5: **Cropping Pattern: Banaskantha and Gujarat**

*(Area in '00 ha.)*

| *Crops.* | *Banaskantha* | *Gujarat* |
|---|---|---|
| Total Pulses | 706 | 9156 |
| | (7.71) | (8.37) |
| Total food grains | 5925 | 52941 |
| | (11.19) | (39.23) |
| Total food crops | 6244 | 67316 |
| | (9.30) | (52.20) |
| Total fodder | 1638 | 9400 |
| | (17.43) | (8.59) |
| Total non-fooder crops | 3695 | 52842 |
| | (6.09) | (48.28) |
| Gross cropped area | | 109448 |

*Source*: Directorate of Agriculture, Govt. of Gujarat, 1984.
*Note*: Figures in brakets are percentages to total.

TABLE 2.6: **Productivity of Selected Food-Crops: Banaskantha and Gujarat**

*(Kg.ha.)*

| *Food crops* | *Banaskantha* | *Gujarat* |
|---|---|---|
| Rice | 760 | 1018 |
| Jowar | 246 | 358 |
| Bajri | 290 | 706 |
| Maize | 741 | 1005 |
| Wheat | 2507 | 2255 |
| Total cereals | 516 | 970 |
| Total pulses | 449 | 616 |
| Total food grains | 508 | 908 |

*Source*: Directorate of Agriculture, Govt. of Gujarat, 1984.

TABLE 2.7: **Land Use Pattern in Banaskantha and Gujarat**

*(area in '00 ha)*

| *Land use pattern* | *Banaskantha* | *Gujarat* |
|---|---|---|
| 1. Total geographical area | 12703 (6.48) | 196008 |
| 2. Reporting area | 12327 (6.55) | 188288 |
| 3. Forest | 1457 (7.41) | 19657 |
| 4. Barren & Uncultivable land | 319 (1.25) | 25596 |
| 5. Land put to non-agri. use | 680 (6.28) | 10811 |
| 6. Permanent pasture & other grazing land | 696 (8.24) | 8450 |
| 7. Cultivable waste | 310 (1.56) | 19889 |
| 8. Current fallow | 507 (6.98) | 7259 |
| 9. Net area sown | 8353 (8.72) | 95831 |
| 10. Area soen more than once | 1581 (11.61) | 13617 |
| 11. Gross cropped area | 9939 (9.08) | 109448 |
| 12. Area not available for cultivation | 999 (2.74) | 36407 |
| 13. Other uncultivable area | 696 (8.20) | 8491 |

*Source*: Directorate of Agri. Govt. of Gujarat, 1984.
*Note*: Figures in brackets are percentage to total.

TABLE 2.8: **Distribution of Land Holdings: Banaskantha and Gujarat**

| *Land size class (in ha.)* | *District/ State* | *No. of holdings* | *%* | *Area of operational holdings (in lac ha.)* | *%* | *Average size of holding* |
|---|---|---|---|---|---|---|
| 0.01-1.00 | Banaskantha | 19037 | (11.73) | 10729 | (1.27) | 0.56 |
| | Gujarat | 710492 | (24.24) | 375961 | (3.72) | 0.53 |
| 1.01-2.00 | Banaskantha | 25752 | (15.87) | 38326 | (4.43) | 1.49 |
| | Gujarat | 634538 | (21.66) | 929557 | (9.20) | 1.46 |
| 2.01-4.00 | Banskantha | 39380 | (24.24) | 114557 | (13.25) | 2.91 |
| | Gujarat | 729701 | (24.84) | 2083477 | (20.62) | 2.86 |
| 4.01-10.0 | Banaskantha | 54737 | (33.70) | 349665 | (40.38) | 6.39 |
| | Gujarat | 685559 | (23.40) | 4209104 | (41.66) | 6.14 |
| 10.01 and above | Banaskantha | 23509 | (14.46) | 352400 | (40.70) | 14.99 |
| | Gujarat | 171639 | (5.86) | 2506129 | (24.80) | 14.60 |

*Source*: Agricultural Census 1980-81. Government of Gujarat.

TABLE 2.9: **Main and Marginal Workers: Banaskantha & Gujarat**

| *Workers* | | *Banaskantha* | *Gujarat* |
|---|---|---|---|
| Main Workers | M | 52.59 | 52.19 |
| | F | 6.75 | 11.03 |
| | T | 30.31 | 32.23 |
| Marginal workers | M | 0.65 | 0.72 |
| | F | 10.77 | 9.63 |
| | T | 5.57 | 5.04 |

*Source*: Directorate Census Operations, Gujarat.

TABLE 2.10: **Average size of Holdings: Banaskantha and Gujarat**

*(in ha.)*

| *Year* | *Banaskantha* | *Gujarat* |
|---|---|---|
| 1970-71 | 6.25 | 4.11 |
| 1976-77 | 5.66 | 3.71 |
| 1980-81 | 5.33 | 3.45 |

*Source*: Directorate of Agriculture, Govt. of Gujarat.

TABLE 2.11: **Pattern of Land Ownership in Gujarat**

| *Size class of land holdings (in ha.)* | *1970-71* | | *1976-77* | | *1980-81* | |
|---|---|---|---|---|---|---|
| | *No. of holdings %* | *Area owned %* | *No. of holding %* | *Area owned %* | *No. of holdings %* | *Area owned %* |
| 0.01 - 1.00 | 23.78 | 3.07 | 24.16 | 3.26 | 24.24 | 3.27 |
| 1.01 - 2.00 | 19.08 | 6.81 | 19.95 | 7.86 | 21.66 | 9.20 |
| 2.01 - 4.00 | 22.81 | 15.97 | 24.02 | 18.57 | 24.84 | 20.62 |
| 4.01 - 10.00 | 24.71 | 37.67 | 24.72 | 41.25 | 23.40 | 41.66 |
| More than 10.01 | 9.62 | 36.48 | 7.15 | 29.06 | 5.86 | 24.80 |

*Source*: Directorate of Agriculture, Govt. of Gujarat.

# PHOTOGRAPHS

PLATE 1: Village Temple on the top of the hill suffered most during the Last Monsoon (Pansha).

PLATE 2: Collection of offerings of Devotees on top of the hill (Mahuda).

PLATE 3: Typical Cattle-shed and storage of fodder (Sembalpani) (Two Photos).

PLATE 4: Drawingroom-cum-verandha with a typical Cot and Earthern Waterpots (Sembalpani).

PLATE 5: Outside view of typical House of Bhilgarasia (Sembalpani)

PLATE 6: Life inside the tribal house. Traditional Grinding-stone used for getting flour and bamboo basket used as craddle to give comforts to child.

PLATE 7: Two different forms of foodgrains storage.

PLATE 8: Lift irrigation being modernised replacing wood by cement concrete.

PLATE 9: Cattle population in search of Grass (Two Photos).

PLATE 9 A: Cattle population in search of Grass (Two Photos).

PLATE 10: Sheep and Cattle rearing as an important subsdiary economic activity of the tribals.

PLATE 11: Guggal — An important forest product of the region finds a retail outlet at Ambaji.

PLATE 12 Forest cover on way to Panshà.

PLATE 13: Lowering density of plants and overcutting of trees at different levels (Pansha).

PLATE 14 Scattered Houses along the foothill region (Mahuda).

PLATE 15 Old banyan tree has survived the Onslaught of Mankind (Pansha).

PLATE 16 Head load of wood on its way to Ambaji market.

PLATE 17 Village deity on the top of the hill (Pansa) (Refer Plate 1 for situation).

PLATE 18 Aged Bhil-Garasia woman reluctantly faced our cameraman.

PLATE 19 Old and new technology remain juxtaposed.

PLATE 20 Hallow basin like wood made out of tree trunk is used for transporting lifted water from the well.

PLATE 21 Extensive use of wood as house building material.

PLATE 22 Peeled bamboo pieces are tied together to make doors inside the house.

PLATE 23 Despite physical and socio-economic adversities young ones are lively (Mahuda).

PLATE 24 Forest products of the region are marketed through Government Contractors.

# INDEX